Leonard Julius Shadwell

Lockhart's Advance through Tirah

Leonard Julius Shadwell

Lockhart's Advance through Tirah

ISBN/EAN: 9783744757652

Printed in Europe, USA, Canada, Australia, Japan

Cover: Foto ©ninafisch / pixelio.de

More available books at **www.hansebooks.com**

LOCKHART'S ADVANCE THROUGH TIRAH.

THE FORT AT SARAGARHI.

BY

CAPT. L. J. SHADWELL, P.S.C.
(SUFFOLK REGIMENT),
Special Correspondent of "The Pioneer" and London "Daily News."

With Two Maps and Seven Full=page Illustrations.

LONDON:
W. THACKER & CO., 2, CREED LANE, E.C.
CALCUTTA: THACKER, SPINK & CO.
1898.

LONDON:
PRINTED BY WILLIAM CLOWES AND SONS, Limited,
STAMFORD STREET AND CHARING CROSS.

PREFACE.

It is with the greatest diffidence that I venture to submit this account of the Advance through Tirah to the public approval, for I can lay no claim to any literary skill or experience. Moreover, I was obliged to write the whole work on board ship, with nothing to assist me beyond a few notes made during the expedition, and I therefore trust that due allowances will be made for the shortcomings of the book.

The incidents in a campaign, and even in a single action, are so numerous and manifold that it would exceed the capabilities of any one person to notice more than an infinitesimal portion of

Preface.

them. I had, however, the advantage of being assisted with the personal observations of a large number of officers, both military and political. It would be quite impossible to mention all those to whose kindness I was in this respect indebted, but I may, perhaps, single out Major-General Lord Methuen, the Press censor with the force, who frequently gave me useful information in addition to that I already possessed, and who on several occasions placed his own notes at my disposal. Particularly was this the case after the action at Dargai on the 20th of October

I have attempted, to the best of my ability, to record the main features of the campaign in a clear and conscientious manner, though I am aware of the fact that I have been unable to do full justice to the splendid courage shown by the officers and men of our British and native troops. If, however, my efforts have enabled the reader to obtain an approximate idea of the actual dangers and hardships that Her Majesty's soldiers cheerfully undergo when on active service in India, I shall feel that my time and labour have not been altogether wasted.

L. J. SHADWELL,
Captain, Suffolk Regt.

February, 1898.

LIST OF CONTENTS.

CHAPTER		PAGE
I.	Brief Description of the Afridi and Orakzai Tribes.	1
II.	Events which led up to the Expedition	27
III.	Base and Lines of Communication	45
IV.	The Transport	68
V.	English as compared with Indian Organisations, and European as compared with Savage Warfare	88
VI.	Preparations for the Advance and the First Action of Dargai	108
VII.	The Attack on Dargai on the 20th October	129
VIII.	The Move into the Khanki Valley, and the Assault of the Sampagha and Arhanga Passes	147
IX.	Description of Afridi Tirah. The Afridis' Guerilla Tactics	171
X.	Events in Camp Maidan, and the Actions on the 9th and 16th November	191
XI.	Move to Bagh. Expeditions to Dwatoi and Esor	224
XII.	The March down the Bara and Mastura Valleys	252
XIII.	Results of the Expedition and Future Policy	295

LIST OF MAPS AND ILLUSTRATIONS

PAGE

MAP OF THE N.W. FRONTIER OF INDIA, SHOWING
    SCENE OF OPERATIONS . . . . . *Facing Chap. I.*
MAP OF THE ROUTE TRAVERSED BY SIR W. LOCKHART
    THROUGH TIRAH . . . *End of book.*
THE FORT AT SARAGARHI . . . . *Frontispiece.*
BOAT BRIDGE ON THE INDUS 46
THE COMMISSARIAT DEPÔT, KOHAT . . 64
THE FATAL RIDGE AT DARGAI 108
THE DARGAI POSITION—FROM ENEMY'S SIDE . 130
VIEW DOWN CHAGRU KOTAL VALLEY . . . 190
A GORGE BETWEEN FORT LOCKHART AND KARAPPA . 252

7

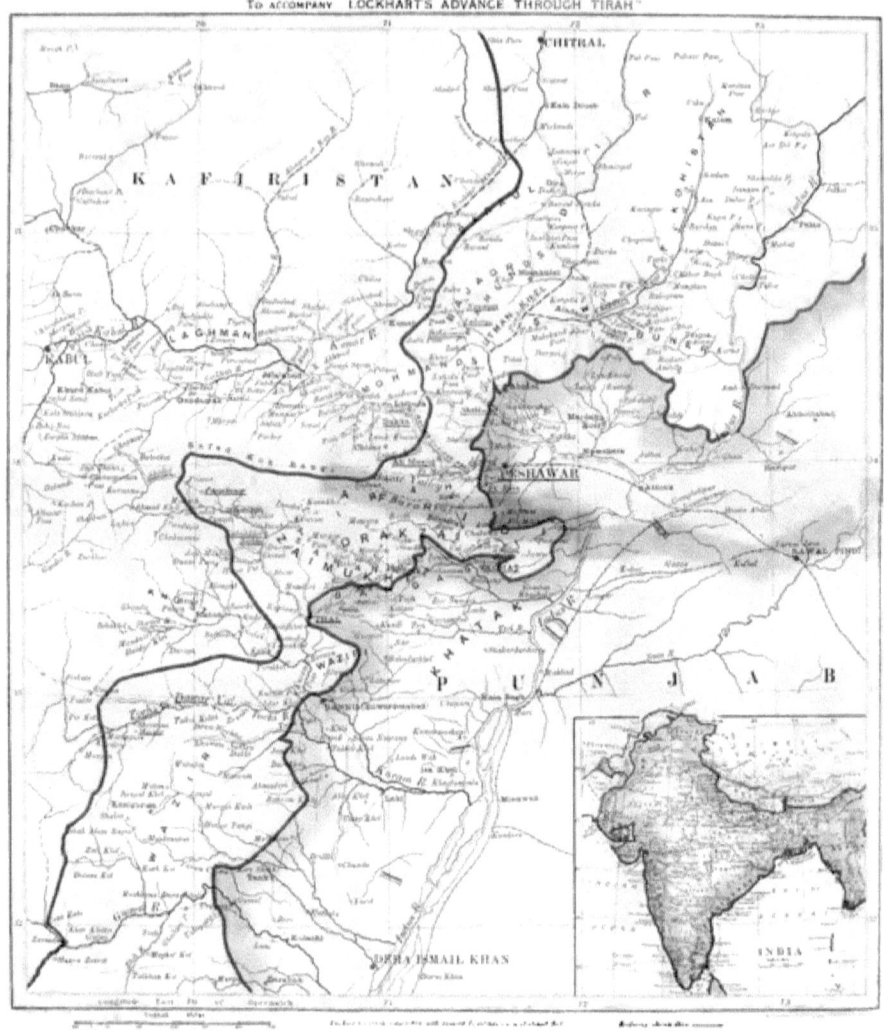

LOCKHART'S
ADVANCE THROUGH TIRAH.

CHAPTER I.

BRIEF DESCRIPTION OF THE AFRIDI AND ORAKZAI TRIBES.

BEFORE entering on a description of the campaign in Tirah, it may be as well to give a very brief description of the Afridi and Orakzai tribes, and of the causes which led to an expedition being sent against them in October 1897 by the Government of India.

Of all the Pathan tribes dwelling on the north-west frontier of India, the Afridis are the most numerous, powerful, and possibly the most warlike.

Roughly speaking, they may be said to occupy a portion of country bounded on the north by the snowy range of the Safed Koh; on the east by the British territory between Peshawur and Kohat and by the Khyber River; on the south and west by the

Orakzai country and by offshoots from the Safed Koh range.

The Afridis are subdivided into eight clans, six of whom are termed Khyber Afridis, because their winter residence is in the country round about the Khyber Pass, and notably in the Bazar Valley; their summer residence being in Tirah, or in the case of one clan of the six—viz., the Kuki Khels—in the Rajgul Valley. Of the other two tribes, the Aka Khels inhabit Waran, a valley south of the Bara River and east of Maidan; while the remaining tribe, the Adam Khels, chiefly inhabit the district between Peshawur and Kohat, and hold the Kohat Pass, through which most of our troops marched from Peshawur in order to concentrate at Kohat.

The fighting strength of the Adam Khel tribe is about six thousand, and the whole of this tribe remained faithful to us through the expedition to Tirah, with the exception of a small and unimportant section who inhabit Tirah, and whose fighting strength is under one thousand men.

It was of great importance that the Adam Khel Afridis, who hold the Kohat Pass, should remain friendly; for, although they receive a yearly subsidy from the Indian Government for the safety of the Kohat Pass road, so widespread were the disturbances on the north-western frontier, that it was feared in some quarters that they might yield to persuasion and throw in their lot with the remainder of the Afridi tribe. Fortunately, however, the Indian Government possessed in Mr. Donald, their political officer at Kohat, a person of immense influence not only over the various Orakzai tribes, but also over the Adam Khel Afridis. In fact, it was in a large measure owing to his influence that the latter held to their contract with the Indian Government, and that our troops passed unmolested from Peshawur through the Kohat Pass.

To return to the remaining Afridi tribes; their total fighting strength, not including the friendly Adam Khels, amounts probably to about twenty-five thousand men, and no tribesmen on the north-western frontier of India are of finer physique or better armed.

The origin of the Afridi race is very obscure. Whereas one writer maintains that they are the descendants of a Jew who embraced the Mahommedan faith, Surgeon-Major Bellew, on the other hand, states that they are without doubt the present representatives of the Aparytae of Herodotus. But they hold only a small portion of the territory owned by their ancestors, having been ousted from the plains by successive invaders, and gradually driven up into the mountainous country which they now inhabit.

Both the Afridis and the Orakzais are divided into two political factions known as Samal and Gar; the Samal or Saman being originally Buddhists, and the Gar or Gabr being Magians. It is supposed that the whole tribe, both Afridis and Orakzais, were at one time forcibly converted to Islam, and called Mussulmans, but that they nevertheless retained, at the time of their forcible conversion, some traces of their early religion, the original Buddhists becoming Samals and the Magians Gars. The same writer, Surgeon-Major Bellew, remarks that the people themselves are absolutely ignorant as to the origin of the Samal and Gar factions in which they have now enrolled themselves; and some authorities, such as Paget and Mason, state that these political factions owed their origin to the quarrel of two brothers bearing those names, and have ever since been at enmity.

However much various writers may differ as to the original history of the Afridis, they nearly all agree as to the following characteristics of the race, characteristics which, as regards their moral attributes, have made the Afridi a by-word even amongst the other Pathans of the north-west frontier.

In appearance the Afridis are tall, wiry, mountaineers, and they can move over the boulders on a precipitous mountain-side with the quickness and surefootedness of a goat. Their complexion, for Orientals, is fair; and they have generally high cheekbones. They wear coarse cotton clothes, which, whatever their original colour may have been, are generally, from want of washing, of the hue of the surrounding rocks and soil—a sort of yellow-grey hue. They wear, as a rule, a sort of grass shoe or sandal made up of dried grass or hay, and are invariably armed, in addition to their rifles, or matchlocks, with one or more knives, stuck in their waistbelts; and if their firearms are not breechloaders, they carry quaint leather powder-flasks, bullet-bags, etc., hung about them.

As regards religion, though professedly a "Sunni" Mahommedan, the Afridi knows little; and he cares still less for the tenets and doctrines of the faith he professes. It is probably only when religion forms an excuse for plunder and breach of faith, as it did in August 1897, that an Afridi considers himself in any way bound by the Koran.

So much so is this the case, that as Surgeon-Major Bellew relates, their barbarism, and their ignorance of the tenets of their religion, made them a laughing-stock and by-word amongst their better instructed neighbours; and so little reverence was shown by the Afridis for any mullah (or Mahommedan priest) who ventured among them, that no mullah dared to enter their country, because of the certainty of being robbed and ill-treated.

The story goes, however, that, shamed by the constant taunts of the neighbouring tribes, they decided on setting up a priest of their own; and with some difficulty induced a too-confiding mullah to come and settle amongst them.

The newly-installed mullah began by impressing on his flock the great religious advantages to be gained from making pilgrimages to the sacred shrines of saints and martyrs, and from the offerings made thereon in the name of the saint. The idea of pilgrimages and offerings seemed acceptable to the reconverted Afridis, but as they had no shrines or burying places of saints in their own country, it seemed a pity that their offerings should be made at a shrine in their neighbours' territory. They determined, therefore, to establish one in their own country, and, as a martyr was required, the newly-arrived mullah was sacrificed. Thus, Tirah had a shrine of its own: though history does not relate if the pious Afridis made it the depositary of offerings.

There were other difficulties, too, in the way of visiting sacred shrines which were not in their own territory; all the surrounding tribes were hostile to the Afridis, and much as the latter love fighting nominally for the sake of religion, still, if no plunder or other advantages were to be gained from it, fighting was not on the whole profitable.

For this reason, to sacrifice the newly-arrived

mullah in order to have a shrine or tomb of a holy man in their own country, was a very simple way out of the difficulty : and it was presumably hoped that the teaching of the departed mullah would induce the more pious-minded among the Afridis to live and die as holy men ; and that by the erection of similar monuments to the memory of departed worthies Tirah might be able to compete with the neighbouring territories in the matter of "ziyarats" or sacred shrines.

Possibly, however, the imported mullah was not allowed a sufficiently long lease of life to admit of his teaching sinking deep into the hearts of his hearers, before his throat was cut in the interests of religion. To this day, the Afridis are generally accounted by their neighbours as indifferent Mahommedans, and Bellew, writing in 1880, remarks : " The Afridi of to-day, though professedly a Mahommedan, has really no religion at all. He is to a great extent ignorant of the tenets and doctrines of the creed he professes ; and even if he knew them, would in no way be restrained by them in the pursuit of his purpose.

" Whatever he may have been as a Buddhist,

or as a fire-worshipper, he has now sunk to the lowest grade of civilization and borders upon the savage. Entirely illiterate, under no acknowledged control, each man his own king, the nation has dwindled down to a small community of less than three hundred thousand souls, mostly robbers and cut-throats, without principles of conduct of any kind, and with nothing but the incentive of the moment as the prompter to immediate action."

Although in some minor particulars the estimate formed by Bellew of the Afridi character differs from that of Paget and Mason in their " Record of the Expeditions against the North-West Frontier Tribes," still, in the main, their estimates agree, as the following quotation from this latter work will show : " Ruthless, cowardly robbery ; treacherous murder, are to an Afridi the salt of life. Brought up from his earliest childhood amid scenes of appalling treachery and merciless revenge, nothing can ever change him ; as he has lived, a shameless, cruel savage, so he dies ; and it would seem that, notwithstanding their long intercourse with the British, and the fact that very large numbers of them have been or are in our service, and must have learnt in some poor way what faith and mercy and justice are, yet the Afridi character is no better than it was in the days of his fathers."

For years past the Afridis have enlisted in the Indian army in large numbers, and many officers who have had to do with them consider them to be excellent soldiers. They show the greatest bravery and *élan* in the attack, and much has been said of their willingness to fight, even when, in some expeditions, regiments, or units, containing a large proportion of Afridis have been called on to attack villages or positions, with the certainty that some at all events of the rank and file of the regiment would have to fire on their own kinsmen or relatives. Their attachment to their officers and the British Government has been greatly lauded by some writers on this account, but as Paget and Mason remark, "When it is remembered that an Afridi generally has a blood-feud with nine out of ten of his own people, the beauty of this attachment fades."

The fact remains, however, that there are numerous instances on record where Afridi native officers and men have been "true to their salt," to use an Oriental expression, under the most trying circumstances; and in that most delightful book, "Across the Border,," by E. E. Oliver, an instance is recorded of an Afridi soldier whose regiment was engaged in hostilities against a village where his own father was in the ranks against him. He urged the British officer to at once commence the fight and not wait till the next day, so that the Afridis in the regiment, whose blood was up, should be relieved of all temptation to desert over night to their relatives and friends.

The Afridi loves a fight, more especially if he is likely to be on the winning side, or if there is any chance of robbery and plunder; but, like some other nations who possess great *élan* and dash on the offensive, it is more than probable that he could not be relied on to the same extent on the defensive, or when the odds seemed against him.

One reason, no doubt, why the campaign in Tirah became so protracted was that the young bloods among the Afridis suddenly awoke to the fact that, although the huge force brought against them rendered organized resistance in a stand-up fight an impossibility, nevertheless unexampled opportunities had arisen for practising guerilla warfare. By firing from long and safe distances into concentrated bodies of the invading force; by cutting up stray and unarmed camp-followers; by attacking convoys, if the escort seemed inadequate, they covered themselves with glory. By capturing the animals and their loads, or shooting an isolated native or, better still, a British soldier, and thus, before his comrades could get to him, capturing the highly-prized Martini or Lee-Metford rifle, they earned wealth.

The maximum of plunder and damage with the minimum of risk seems the motto of the Afridi warrior, and when it is remembered that the value of a Martini-Henry rifle across the border is about four hundred rupees, or, say, £27, and that of a Lee-Metford possibly still more, and that the possession of one or the other would very likely enable its fortunate owner to successfully shoot his hereditary enemy, whose house had hitherto been out of range from his own dwelling, can we wonder that the young men of the Afridis and Orakzais, unhampered by wives and families, and, unlike their elders, thinking more of present advantages and excitement than of ruin and famine in the future, should be averse to the conclusion of peace. It would not only mean an end to the plunder and bloodshed, but might, far worse than this, entail the headmen of the tribe calling on them to hand in the much-prized rifle to make up the number of arms demanded by the British Government as part of the terms to be complied with before the country was evacuated.

In most disturbances on the north-western frontier of India it is doubtless often the desire of the greybeards amongst the tribesmen to avoid all hostile acts against the British, for long experience has taught them that the Indian Government will enact reprisals and enforce terms, the after effects of which will be felt for years. But the young men, who see, or who think they see, a chance for successful robbery and murder, commit some overt hostile act, under the instigation of a pestilential mullah, and afterwards drag with them the formerly unwilling elder men of the tribe. Once blood has been shed, it is then very difficult for any Pathan, old or young, to hold aloof.

A great deal of mischief, too, is often caused by the mullahs or priests, who frequently try and inflame the warlike passions of a tribe for their own selfish ends, and to increase their reputation and income. In this respect they scarcely resemble the "Poure Persoun of a town" so much praised by Chaucer, who—

> ". . . . ranne not to Londone unto St. Powle's
> To seeken him a Chauntrie for sowles,
> Or with a Bretherhed to ben withholde,
> But stayed at home and kepte well his folde,
> So that the wolfe ne made it not miscarie.
> He was a shepherde and no mercenarie."

Too often, it is to be feared, the frontier mullah is much more of a "mercenarie" than a "shepherde," and the easiest means for him to obtain preferment to the Mahommedan equivalent of a "Chauntrie for sowles," or a canonry, is for him to preach a "jihad," or religious war, and thus acquire a notoriety and an increased income among the tribesmen.

Paget and Mason, the authors of the "Record of Expeditions against the North-West Frontier Tribes," aver that the men among the Afridis do little or no domestic work, and that, when not engaged in plundering, time hangs very heavily on their hands; their women cut the wood, fetch the water, and do nearly all the outdoor labour in the fields. It is probably the case that the women do all the work connected with the household, but till the expedition under Sir William Lockhart entered Tirah, no one apparently had any idea that the Orakzais, in the Mastura Valley, and the Afridis, in Maidan, lived in such large, commodious, and solidly built houses, or that the ground was so highly cultivated as it was found to be.

The women alone—however unwomanly they may be—could never have erected such houses or cultivated the ground and cut out terraces and channels for irrigation purposes, unaided by the men; though they probably assist largely in all outdoor work.

Paget and Mason compute that there are between three thousand and four thousand Afridis in military service, either under the British Government or the native chiefs in India. And it will be interesting to see whether, after the Afridis have complied with the terms of the Indian Government and peace is concluded, they will continue to offer themselves for enlistment in such large numbers as hitherto.

Of all the Afridi tribes, the Zakka Khels bear the worst reputation as soldiers; not that they are less brave, but because they are reputed to be the greatest rifle thieves on the frontier; and very few, if any, native regiments serving on or near the north-west frontier will enlist Zakka Khels at all.

Regiments in the Bombay Presidency do so to some extent, probably because it is not easy to enlist Afridis of other clans. The latter naturally prefer to serve nearer home, as would the Zakka Khels, if they were given the opportunity.

Another reason which minimises the risk of enlisting Zakka Khel Afridis further down country, is that it would be extremely difficult for them to desert with their rifles and ammunition when so far away from the frontier. For so great is the desire of an Afridi to possess a good firearm, that if he cannot save up his money and buy one, or cross the frontier and steal one, he will try to enlist in a native regiment, with the sole object of eventually deserting with his rifle.

Taking these things into consideration, it is

astonishing how comparatively few Afridis do desert and carry away their arms. Possibly this is due in a small measure to the fact that the arms of all men not on duty are locked up at night; but probably still more to the great discrimination shown by the officers commanding the native regiments who enlist Afridis, and who very often hold other Afridis in the regiment responsible for any of their friends or relations whom they recommend as recruits, and will not accept a man for whom no one can answer.

In the cold weather the Afridis, and more especially those in the Kohat Pass, do a large business in British territory, by bringing in wood for sale,—for which, especially in the large cantonment of Peshawur, there is a great demand; they also carry away salt, not only for use in their own territory, but in that inhabited by other border tribes. In former days, when an Afridi clan misbehaved itself, a strict blockade, preventing as it did their entering British territory for trading purposes, was generally sufficient to bring the clansmen to their senses.

It is a remarkable thing that the Afridis have

for generations had Hindoos, but of the Sikh religion, living amongst them. The Mahommedan has such an aversion to idolatry in any form that the Sikhs, who are not idolaters, are the only Hindoos he could tolerate; and to these Hindoos is consigned much of the trade. It is difficult to ascertain exactly the position that these Sikhs hold in the Afridi villages; but they appear to be the grain dealers, the middlemen in trade matters, and very possibly, in so far as drawing up mortgages and deeds of sale of land, the lawyers.

These Sikhs are compelled to wear a particular dress to distinguish them from Mahommedans, and each Sikh has a certain Mahommedan who acts as his patron or guardian, and who exercises certain feudal rights by exacting tribute from him and his family.

As regards blood-feuds, some of these have existed between various families for generations, and some are of later date; most frequently they arise from quarrels about women. Whatever may be the cause, all Pathans (under which term are included all the independent tribes on the north-west frontier of India who are not Biluchis) regard the prosecution of a blood-feud as the one great aim and object in life, and few or none of them are without a blood-feud of some sort.

A Pathan who is not rich enough to buy a good rifle, or skilful enough to go and steal it in British territory, will enlist into a regiment with the sole object of eventually acquiring a good one. Having saved sufficient money, he will then apply for furlough with the almost avowed object of going home to try and shoot his enemy. In "Across the Border, or Pathan and Biluch" it is related how an Afridi soldier who had asked, as a great favour, from a British officer for a little sporting powder before proceeding on furlough, returned at the end of his leave from across the border, and informed the donor that his powder was excellent, and had enabled him to accomplish the end he had in view.

Sometimes a blood-feud is by mutual consent allowed to slumber for years, more particularly if the enemies are not near neighbours. And Paget and Mason remark that very frequently a Pathan. whose ancestors have bequeathed him many blood-feuds, is glad to escape to the haven of India, and the rest afforded by military service; for possibly when he returns, death, or time, or other reasons, may have diminished the number of feuds, and thus afford him an opportunity of more successfully prosecuting the important ones that remain. Tribal feuds also exist to some extent in addition to family feuds, and in this case any one of the tribe implicated is liable to be shot by a perfect stranger of the other tribe. Thus tribal life in the Afridi and Orakzai country is not altogether without its excitement.

It may be well now to turn to the Orakzais.

The country they inhabit is bounded on the north and east by the Afridi country, on the south by the Miranzai Valley, and on the west by the Zaimukt country and branches from the Safed Koh Range.

The Orakzais number about twenty-five thousand fighting men; and are divided into six main clans, which are again subdivided into twenty-one sections.

Roughly speaking, about one half the Orakzais belong, politically, to the Samal, and the other half to the Gar faction; and while most of them are Sunni Mahommedans, a considerable number are Shiah Mahommedans, so that not only are there often political but religious feuds as well.

When the terms of the Indian Government had been announced at Maidan to the assembled Orakzai "jirgahs," or representative deputations, a dispute arose between the Samal and Gar factions as to how the fine was to be apportioned between them. The adherents of these two factions returned to seek the advice of the political officer on the point, and he suggested that as the Samal faction was about equal in numbers to the Gar, the former should pay half the indemnity, and the latter the other half. This simple solution of the difficulty did not appear to have occurred to the unaided Orakzai intellect.

The Orakzais pay somewhat more attention to religious matters than the Afridis, and are very superstitious; their religious leaders, therefore, exert a good deal of influence among them.

The name Tirah is collectively given to those high open valleys from which rise the two streams forming the Bara River, and also those streams which form the Khanki and Kurmana rivers. It is an area of six hundred or seven hundred square miles in extent. Of this, the Afridi Tirah is the highland through which the Bara River flows— the Maidan, Rajgul and upper Bara valleys. These are the summer quarters of the Afridi tribes. The rest of the Tirah is Orakzai country.

The latter tribe have not the same martial reputation as the Afridis, but Macgregor states:— "No one doubts that an Orakzai, as much as any Pathan, would shrink from no falsehood, however atrocious, to gain his end. Money would buy his services for the foulest deed, cruelty of the most revolting kind would mark his actions to a fallen or a helpless foe." This estimate of the Orakzai character, written some years ago, was singularly borne out by the attack they made on the garrisons of the Gulistan and Saragarhi forts in August, 1897, and by the indignities they offered to the corpses of the gallant Sikh defenders of the last-named post—events to which I shall allude in the next chapter.

The Orakzais are not on the whole such a wealthy tribe as the Afridis, and consequently not quite so well armed. Some sections of the tribe, whose country is in the low-lying ground, and not in far-off Tirah, have always been open to attack if the Indian Government wished to effect reprisals for any raid, as is the case with those who cultivate the open Miranzai Valley in the winter. But some sections of the tribes living in remote Tirah could only be punished indirectly—by proclaiming a strict blockade, and not allowing them to trade with British India—unless, of course, as in 1897, a force large enough to overcome all possible resistance was sent against them. Several small expeditions against various sections of the Orakzais have from time to time been successfully brought to a conclusion, but Tirah proper has never been penetrated till the present expedition entered it.

Most of what I have said regarding the Afridis applies equally to the Orakzais, and as these two nations are the most numerous and powerful of all the Pathan tribes inhabiting the north-west frontier of India, I cannot, I think, better conclude this chapter than by quoting from a report written in 1855 by Mr. Temple, as he then was, in his capacity as Secretary to the Chief Commissioner of the Punjaub, with reference to the frontier tribes. No better summary of the Pathan character has, perhaps, ever been written, and though over forty years have elapsed, the Pathan characteristics remain unchanged.

"Now these tribes," he says, "are savages—noble savages, perhaps, and not without some tincture of virtue and generosity—but still absolutely barbarians nevertheless. They have nothing approaching to government or civil institutions; they have, for the most part, no education. They have nominally a religion, but Mahommedanism, as understood by them, is no better, but perhaps is actually worse, than the creeds of the wildest race on earth. In their eyes the one great commandment is blood for blood, and fire and sword for all infidels; that is, for all people not Mahommedans. They are superstitious and priest-ridden. But the priests (mullahs) are as ignorant as they are bigoted, and use their influence simply for preaching crusades against unbelievers, and inculcate the doctrine of rapine and bloodshed against the defenceless people of the plain.

"The hillmen are sensitive in regard to their women, but their customs in regard to marriage and betrothal are very prejudicial to social advancement; at the same time they are a sensual race. They are very avaricious for gold; they will do almost anything except betray a guest; they are thievish and predatory to the last degree. The Pathan mother often prays that her son may be a successful robber. They are utterly faithless to public engagements; it would never even occur to their minds that an oath on the Koran was binding if against their interests. It must be added that they are fierce and bloodthirsty.

"They are never without weapons. When grazing their cattle, when driving beasts of burden, when tilling the soil, they are still armed. They are perpetually at war with each other. Every tribe and section of a tribe has its internecine wars, every family its hereditary blood-feuds, and every individual his personal foes. There is hardly a man whose hands are unstained; every person counts up his murders.

"Each tribe has a debtor and creditor account with its neighbours—life for life. Reckless of the lives of others, they are not sparing of their own; they consider retaliation and revenge to be the strongest of all obligations. They possess gallantry and courage themselves, and admire such qualities in others. Men of the same party will stand by one another in danger. To their minds hospitality is the first of virtues. Any person who can make his way into their dwellings will not only be safe, but will be kindly received; but as soon as he has left the roof of his entertainer he may be robbed or killed.

"They are charitable to the indigent of their own tribe. They possess the pride of birth, and regard ancestral associations. They are not averse to civilization, whenever they have felt its benefits. They are fond of trading, and also of cultivating, but they are too fickle and excitable to be industrious in agriculture or anything else. They will take military service, and, though impatient of discipline, will prove faithful, unless excited by fanaticism. Such, briefly, is their character, replete with the unaccountable inconsistencies, with that mixture of opposite vices and virtues, belonging to savages."

CHAPTER II.

THE EVENTS WHICH LED TO THE EXPEDITION.

THE Scheme issued from the office of the Quartermaster-General in India towards the end of September, 1897, and which gave the composition of and other details connected with the Force intended to take part in the Tirah Expedition, contained the following announcement in its first paragraph:—

"The general object of this expedition is to exact reparation for the unprovoked aggression of the Afridi and Orakzai tribes on the Peshawur and Kohat borders, for their attacks on our frontier-posts, and for the damage to life and property which has thus been inflicted on British subjects and on those in the British service.

"It is believed that this object can best be attained by the invasion of Tirah, the summer home of the Afridis and Orakzais, which has never before been entered by a British force."

It will be remembered that the political horizon in India, which seemed so calm and cloudless at the beginning of June, 1897, was suddenly, on the 10th of that month, disturbed at Maizar, when a treacherous attack was made on the escort to a political officer, resulting in the death of three British officers and twenty-three native officers and soldiers, and in three British officers and several men being wounded. To avenge this attack, a punitive expedition into the Tochi Valley was decided on, and early in July the force detailed (about two brigades) started under the command of Major-General Corrie Bird. Matters in the Tochi seemed to be settling down again when, on the 26th July, a sudden and most unexpected attack was made on the garrison of the Malakand and of Chakdara, which adjoins it. These attacks were continued at intervals up till the end of August, and resulted in heavy losses to the garrison and relieving forces, though those incurred by the enemy in their numerous and unsuccessful attacks were very severe indeed, and have been estimated as nearly three thousand.

To avenge these attacks a force of about a

division, termed the Malakand Field Force, and under the command of Br.-General Sir Bindon Blood, was formed for operations in the neighbourhood of the Malakand.

The attacks on the Malakand and Chakdara appeared to have aroused the warlike temper of nearly all the frontier tribes; for, on the 8th of August, the whole of India was astounded by the news that a tribe termed the Mohmands, living in the neighbourhood of Peshawur, had invaded British territory the previous evening and attacked the fort of Shabkadr, garrisoned by border police; and although the attack on Shabkadr fort was unsuccessful, the neighbouring village of Shankargarh was burnt, and those few inhabitants who had not fled into the fort, murdered.

Shabkadr fort is only eighteen miles from Peshawur, and yet, notwithstanding this, the civil authorities at Peshawur were unaware that anything untoward was impending, despite the fact that it was rumoured in the native bazaars two or three days before, that the Mohmands were being incited by the Hadda Mullah to go on the warpath. This and the subsequent attacks on the Khyber by the

Afridis, which were equally unsuspected by the civil and political authorities till shortly before they occurred, enable one to understand how the risings in the Indian Mutiny of 1857 came as a surprise to the Indian authorities of those days. Not only, however, had the impending trouble been rumoured in the bazaars, but the Hindoo grain sellers and money lenders at Shankargarh had in many cases moved into Peshawur several days beforehand, and nearly all the inhabitants of that village had sufficient warning to enable them to move into the adjoining fort of Shabkadr.

A force was at once moved out to Shabkadr when the news of the raid on British territory reached Br.-General Ellis, commanding at Peshawur. The following day the fight of Shabkadr took place, memorable for the brilliant charge of two squadrons of the 13th Bengal Lancers, ordered at a critical moment by General Ellis, when this little force of cavalry under Major Atkinson swept down the whole length of the enemy's line, and threw it into the most complete confusion.

Following on the attack of the Mohmands on Shabkadr, came rumours of disturbances among the

Afridis and Orakzais; and to guard against all eventualities the formation at Rawal Pindi of two reserve brigades (each with cavalry, artillery, and sappers and miners attached) was ordered about the 15th of August.

Br.-General Westmacott was given the command of one of these brigades, Major-General Yeatman-Biggs of the other, and the force at Peshawur under Br.-General Ellis' command was largely augmented.

Rumours regarding the continued action of the Orakzais and Afridis now began to take a more definite shape; and it was stated that, while the Orakzais would raid our posts on the Samana range, the Afridis would simultaneously attack and possess themselves of the Khyber Pass (the forts in which were garrisoned by the Khyber Rifles). Fortunately for us, the Pathan is an eminently distrustful being. Treacherous himself to the last degree, he always expects treachery in his neighbour; and although the Orakzais had undoubtedly promised the Afridis that they would act simultaneously and in concert, they nevertheless, before they took action, waited to see what course the Afridis would pursue. This latter tribe must soon have dispelled all doubts in the minds of its so-called allies, for, on the 23rd of August, a vast number of Afridis attacked the Khyber Forts, defended by their kinsmen and brothers of the Khyber Rifles. By the evening of that day the whole Pass was in the enemy's hands.

Although many rumours had been current as to the date the Afridis would commence hostilities, it was not definitely known at Peshawur till the 21st of August that they had actually begun to move from Tirah; and Br.-General Ellis, commanding at Peshawur, who had now some ten thousand men at his disposal, in addition to the regiments at Jamrud, near the entrance of the Khyber, despatched a column to Fort Bara, some seven miles south-east of Jamrud.

The scheme which has been adopted since 1881 for holding the Khyber Pass was as follows. In that year, which had just seen the close of the Afghan War, and the placing of Abdur Rahman on the throne of Afghanistan, arrangements were entered into with the Khyber Afridis by which they agreed, for a certain yearly sum of money, and in consideration of their independence being guaranteed, to keep open the Khyber Pass on behalf of the British Government. To garrison the forts in the pass, and generally speaking to secure the safety of all travellers and caravans moving through it, an irregular corps of riflemen was formed, termed the Khyber Rifles, and entirely composed of Pathans living in the neighbourhood of the pass. Up till quite lately this corps was commanded by an Afridi native officer, Major Aslam Khan; and under his leadership a strong contingent of the Khyber Rifles gave the regular troops of the Indian army great assistance in the Black Mountain Campaign of 1888.

About eighteen months ago, Captain Barton, of the Guides Cavalry, succeeded Major Aslam Khan as Commandant of the Khyber Rifles, and as political officer in the Khyber. No better appointment could possibly have been made, for Captain Barton most thoroughly understands Pathans, and more especially Afridis, is a thorough master of their language, and knows how to identify himself with the men under his command, so as to win their entire confidence and respect. Captain

Barton, when he heard the news of the attack on Shabkadr, at once anticipated that the fanatical rising might spread to the Afridis, and to be ready for every emergency, laid in fifteen days' food and water supply at Landi Kotal. He also increased the garrison, brought up fifty thousand rounds of ammunition, and determined to remain in the fort himself.

On the 17th of August, or six days before the actual attack was made, he wrote to Sir Richard Udny, the Commissioner of Peshawur, asking him for some regular troops and guns, without which his garrison was quite inadequate to defend the large perimeter of the fort. So far from receiving these reinforcements, however, he was ordered to move into Jamrud, at the mouth of the pass, near Peshawur; and thither he had to go. His belongings, all of which eventually fell into the enemy's hands, he had left behind in the Landi Kotal fort, to which he shortly expected to return.

The Khyber Rifles were thus left to their fate without any British officer to command them. But even so the garrison resisted attack for over twenty-four hours, losing one native officer killed and one wounded, and about ten men. Most of the Khyber Rifles eventually made their way to Jamrud and brought their rifles with them, an incident which speaks volumes for their loyalty to the British Government. There were only about four hundred and fifty men of the Khyber Rifles available for defending the whole of the Khyber Pass, some twenty miles in length, but the political authorities at Peshawur did not deem it advisable to move troops up to their assistance, and the entire pass fell into the hands of the Afridis.

The loss of the Khyber Pass must undoubtedly have affected the prestige of the British Government, not only on the frontier, but throughout India and Afghanistan; and rumour has it that no one was more surprised than the Afridis, when they arrived there and found that none of the posts had been reinforced. It is said they were quite prepared to tell the mullah or priest who had been inciting them to the attack that the task was an impossible one; but the capture of Landi Kotal, with its fifty thousand rounds of ammunition, was a great prize; and once a Pathan's blood is up by dint of successful murder or plunder, it takes him a long time before he can again settle down to peaceful pursuits.

It is now time to turn to the Orakzais. I have said before that, fortunately for us, they did not rise simultaneously with the Afridis, and they thus gave time for troops to be pushed on to Kohat to guard against any movement they might make.

Major-General Yeatman-Biggs had come up from Rawal Pindi and assumed command of all the troops between Kohat and the Kurram. The news of the success achieved by the Afridis in the Khyber probably reached the Orakzais very soon afterwards, for on the night of the 26th August, three days after the Pass had fallen, a levy post near the Ublan Pass, north-west of Kohat, was seized, one man of the garrison being killed, two wounded, and the remainder driven back on Mahomedzai.

Major-General Yeatman-Biggs moved out early on the 27th from Kohat with a small force to attack the enemy, who were holding the Ublan Pass. The heat was very great, and the difficulties in the ascent enormous, but the pass was taken, with the loss of one British soldier, who died of apoplexy, one sepoy killed, one native officer and two sepoys wounded. No water was procurable, nor could mules carrying water accompany the troops. The enemy followed up when the retirement began, killing two men, and wounding two British officers, two native officers and eight men. On the 30th of August a determined attack was made by a large number of tribesmen on Balish Khel post, near Sadda, held by twenty men of the Kurram Militia under an Afridi non-commissioned officer. This gallant little garrison, though their leader was fighting his kinsmen, held out from the tower even after the enemy had forced their way into the enclosure; they were only rescued in the nick of time by a reinforcement of the Kurram Militia that arrived from Sadda.

Still more exciting events now began to take place on the Samana range. After the expedition against the Orakzais of 1891, three outlying posts or small forts had been established on this range, viz., Fort Lockhart, Fort Saragarhi, and Fort Gulistan or Cavagnari. Fort Saragarhi had only been constructed as a signalling post between Forts

Lockhart and Gulistan, which are hidden from one another by an intervening hill.

On the 12th of September an overwhelming number of tribesmen surrounded the little fort of Saragarhi, the garrison of which consisted of twenty-one sepoys of the 36th Regiment of Sikhs.

This magnificent regiment, of which Lieutenant-Colonel Haughton was then in command, was only raised some ten years ago, and this was the first campaign in which it had taken part. The grand way in which its men have fought, not only on the Samana Range, but all through the expedition in Tirah, has now made it one of the most distinguished regiments in the Indian Army; but its losses, especially in British officers, have been very heavy, and culminated at the end of January, 1898, in the death of their gallant leader, Lieutenant-Colonel Haughton, and of his acting adjutant, Lieutenant Turing.

Between Sikhs and Pathans there has for time out of mind existed the most deadly hatred, born of the day when the Sikhs held the Punjaub and punished, far less mercifully than we ever have done, any raid of the frontier tribes into Sikh territory.

Events which led to the Expedition.

No more stubborn soldier serves Her Majesty in any part of the world than the dignified and faithful Sikh; and although the tribesmen were in overpowering numbers when they surrounded the little garrison of Fort Saragarhi, many a one bit the dust before and even after they had forced an entrance into the fort.

For nearly seven hours this little band of heroes held out; but the fort in which they were, was not calculated to stand such a determined attack as was made upon it, for at the corner of the flanking tower was a dead angle, or in other words, a portion of the wall could not have fire brought to bear on it from any portion of the parapet or from loopholes. One or two of the enemy having crept up to this dead angle managed to loosen a corner stone.

This sealed the fate of the twenty-one Sikhs, for stone after stone fell; and the enemy finally crowded into the fort. But all was not over, even yet; for those of the garrison who were still capable of fighting defended an inner enclosure, till the enemy climbed the wall on all sides. One wounded Sikh lying on a bed shot four of the enemy before he was himself killed, and the last remaining man, having shut himself in the guard-room, accounted for nearly twenty Pathans, till they in desperation set fire to the house. But, true to the Sikh faith, which teaches its followers that no death is more glorious than that obtained when fighting with one's face to the foe, he died in the flames. He thus denied his cruel foes the satisfaction of mutilating his body, a savage act of final brutality which they performed in the case of all the other bodies.

For a photograph of Fort Saragarhi taken after it had been captured and partially destroyed by the tribesmen, see Frontispiece. All the rocks and stones around were bespattered with lead, showing how heavy had been the firing. What is known of the details of the fighting at Saragarhi was chiefly gathered from the accounts of some of the tribesmen who joined in the attack, and from them was learnt the extent of their own losses, and how the last remaining Sikh accounted for twenty Afghans. But not a single Sikh fell alive into their hands.

The garrisons of Forts Lockhart and Gulistan,

the former commanded by Lieutenant-Colonel Haughton, and the latter by Major Des Vœux, had to look on at the capture of Fort Saragarhi without being able to afford any assistance. Both of them attempted to send aid from the very slender garrisons they had at their disposal; but the detachments had to be at once recalled, as the enemy were seen in overwhelming numbers, to be trying to outflank them and cut off their line of retreat. The tribesmen, as soon as they had hemmed in the garrison of Saragarhi, turned their attention to Fort Gulistan or Cavagnari, commanded by Major Des Vœux, who had with him in the little fort his wife, two children, and a nurse, Miss McGrath, whose attentions to the wounded Sikhs throughout the siege were unremitting.

The garrison only numbered one hundred and sixty-five, whilst the enemy surrounding them were estimated at from ten to fifteen thousand, and as the only water supply is some distance from the fort, the privations suffered by the garrison for want of this precious liquid were intense. Major Des Vœux had taken every possible precaution which the short warning he had of the impending attack allowed him to do. A supply of water was laid in, though quite insufficient for more than one day, barricades were constructed, and as far as possible, arrangements made to meet every contingency.

The attack began early on the 12th, and on the morning of the 13th the enemy, taking advantage of a quantity of dead ground, or ground unseen from the fort, had massed in positions close under the walls. A gallant sortie was made by a Sikh sergeant with sixteen men to capture a standard which the enemy had brought up close to the wall, but they were found in great strength, and several of the Sikhs were wounded. Another native sergeant sallying out with more men to the assistance of the first party, the whole force, about twenty-five in number, charged with the bayonet, captured no less than three standards, and brought back all their wounded into the fort. Never has a finer deed of arms than this been accomplished, and its complete success greatly raised the morale of the garrison, and at the same time lowered that of the section of the tribesmen to whom the standards belonged. The hospital in the fort soon became full of wounded, and Surgeon-Captain Prall, of the 36th Sikhs, assisted by Miss McGrath, attended to their wants incessantly, though nothing could make up for the scarcity of water. The little garrison stuck manfully to their posts till about mid-day on the 14th September, when the welcome sound of guns was heard from the direction of Fort Lockhart, and about 2 P.M. a force under General Yeatman-Biggs arrived and relieved the exhausted garrison.

Out of the original force of one hundred and sixty-five, forty-four were killed and wounded, and two followers killed. The stubborn defence made by Major Des Vœux and his gallant Sikhs greatly impressed the unsuccessful tribesmen, for, about two months later, when one of their jirgahs or deputations arrived at Camp Maidan, the first question they asked the political officer was whether the officer who had so successfully defended Fort Gulistan against them had received a medal for his bravery.

Many minor acts of hostility, in addition to those I have mentioned, were performed both by Afridis and Orakzais, such as the seizing and burning of various police-posts, and the investiture of Fort Gulistan by the Orakzais from the 27th August till about the 4th September. But my intention has been to merely touch on the main incidents which formed a "casus belli," and which, as the most pacific reader will admit, rendered reparation inevitable.

Before I close this chapter, I will relate one more incident, which shows better than any description of character, how cruel and ferocious a being the Pathan tribesman is.

On the morning of October the 12th, before the attack on Fort Gulistan had begun, three unarmed followers of the Sikh garrison went out to collect wood. Some three days later their bodies were discovered. They had been tied together and burnt alive!

CHAPTER III.

THE BASE AND LINES OF COMMUNICATION.

BEFORE an army can be concentrated it is necessary to establish what is technically termed a "base of operations." This base of operations must necessarily be situated well out of striking distance of the enemy, so that the work of accumulating supplies of all kinds and munitions of war may proceed uninterruptedly. Another very important point as regards the base of operations being situated well out of striking distance of the enemy, is that it is highly desirable to limit, to as small a number as possible, the number of troops used for the protection of the supplies, and for the work of unloading and arranging them for their onward conveyance. Otherwise a large proportion of the supplies intended for the use of the troops when the forward movement begins, would be used up in feeding those collected at the base. As the troops commence to advance from the base of operations towards the hostile country, depôts for food supply have to be established at various points along the road to be traversed; and this road, together with the various depôts situated on it, is technically termed the "line of communications."

In European warfare the base of operations is generally a large railway centre, and the line of communications frequently a railway, as was the case in the Franco-German war. In the Peninsular War the British base of operations was invariably some seaport, and in the Egyptian campaign of 1882 Ismailia was the base. But in India the base of operations must almost invariably be a place either on a line of railway, such as Peshawur and Quetta, or much more often a place like Kohat, connected with the railway by a metalled road, and thus permitting the use of wheeled as distinct from pack transfer.

So excellent is the disposition of the railways along the north-west frontier of India at the present time, that two termini offered themselves as bases of operations for the Tirah campaign, viz., Peshawur, which is on the main line of the North Western Railway, running from Delhi, viâ

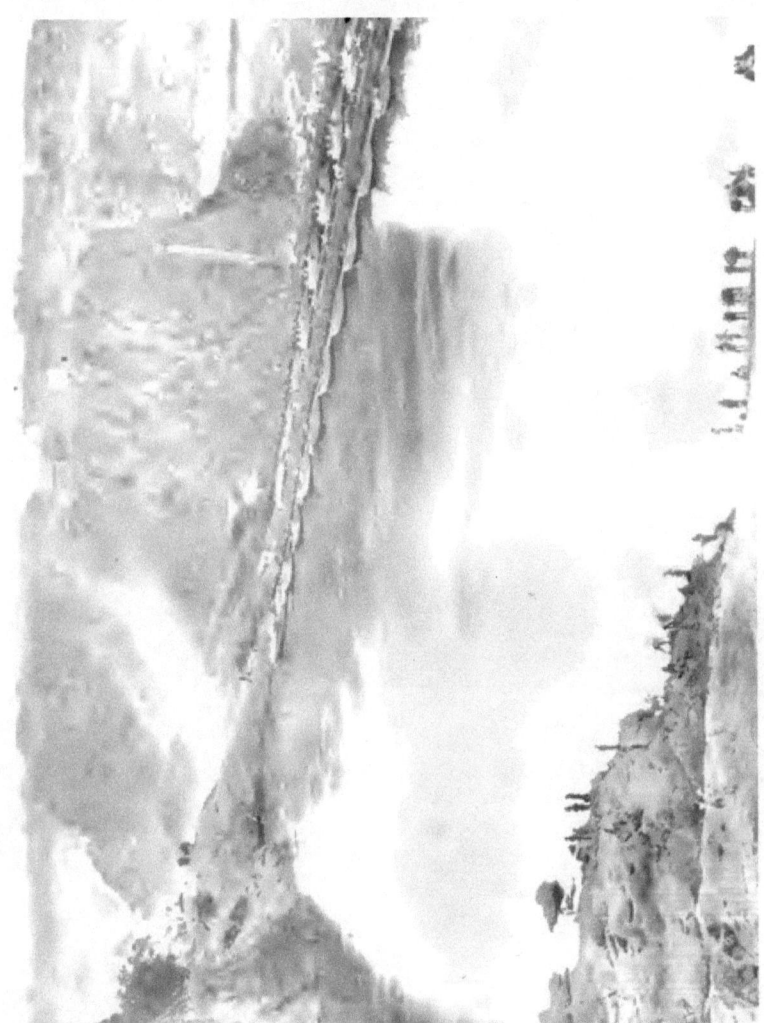

Lahore and Rawal Pindi, and Khusalgarh, the terminus of a small branch line that leaves the main line near Rawal Pindi, and runs out in the direction of Kohat.

I do not propose to discuss at very great length the relative merits of Peshawur and Khusalgarh as bases: the matter has been very warmly debated by various writers in Indian and other newspapers. Suffice it to say that once Shinawari is reached, which is about seven marches by a metalled road from Khusalgarh, an advance viâ the Sampagha and Arhanga Passes takes an invader in three or four marches straight into the heart of the Orakzai and Afridi country, by two very fairly practicable routes.

It must be remembered that the Tirah country was absolutely unknown; and one great advantage in advancing viâ Kohat lay in the fact that the route as far as Karappa, about one march from Shinawari, was to some extent familiar. In a previous campaign conducted by Sir William Lockhart, partly against the Orakzais, Karappa had been visited, though approached from another direction; and that place is within one march only of the Sampagha, the pass leading into Orakzai Tirah. Moreover, the Samana Range, which was already in our possession, and on which Forts Lockhart, Saragarhi, and Gulistan are situated commands a very good view of the Sampagha Pass and of the enemy's preparations for defending it. A force, therefore, advancing from Shinawari and the Samana Range, groped in the dark to a much less extent than one advancing from Peshawur into Tirah would do. On the other hand there was the very serious disadvantage of a long line of communication by road before our force could commence hostilities, and a line, moreover, which was exposed from a few miles after Kohat right up to Shinawari to attacks in flank from the enemy. This portion of the road skirts the Orakzai country, and required a strong force merely to protect it from attacks of this nature.

Peshawur, had it been selected as the base of operations, would have had the advantage of a more convenient railway approach, greater accommodation within the cantonment itself, and a much shorter line of communications to the point where hostile operations against Afridis or Orakzais could begin. But the advance from Peshawur into Tirah lay through unknown and difficult country; and to reach the heart of Afridi Tirah many more marches along difficult mountain-tracks would have been necessary than was the case from Shinawari, to which place a metalled road already existed.

It is true that if the main base of operations had been at Peshawur a force could at once advance from there and strike the Afridis in their settlements in the Bazar Valley, and proceed to open up the Khyber Pass; but it had always been a boast of the Afridis that Tirah, which includes the high-lying valleys and plateaus at an elevation of some six thousand feet, had not only never been entered by any hostile force, but was of so difficult and inaccessible a nature as to practically preclude any operations being undertaken against its inhabitants.

To quote a term used by the Afridis themselves, the Tirah country was "purdah nashin," or concealed behind the curtain. The expression is used by Mahommedans in talking of their women for the wife of a Mahommedan is almost invariably "purdah nashin," that is to say, strictly secluded from the public gaze behind a curtain. "Never," said the Afridis and Orakzais, " has the curtain of Tirah been drawn aside." In the case of Tirah the curtain is formed by the lofty ranges of mountains with difficult passes and precipitous tracks, which surround the country on all sides. The plan of campaign was to concentrate the main column of the Tirah Expedition, consisting of two divisions, at Shinawari, the most advanced post on the metalled road, and thence strike straight into the heart of Tirah. The moral effect of rudely brushing aside the curtain hitherto undrawn would necessarily be great. Some people were of opinion that the concentration of such a large force, ready to sweep aside all opposition and to march into the centre of Tirah, would induce both Orakzais and Afridis to abandon all hope of successful resistance, and accede to whatever terms the Government of India might please to dictate. Others again, and these, I should say, formed the vast majority, thought that both Orakzais and Afridis would fight to defend the passes leading into Tirah, and that they would do so not so much in the hope of successfully resisting our advance as of maintaining their prestige as fighting men among their neighbours, and thus saving themselves from the taunts of their women folk and the other Pathan tribes.

It will be remembered that in the Chitral campaign of 1895 the tribesmen offered battle at the Malakand, and, having received a decisive defeat, practically abandoned all further resistance; and this has been the case in many of the Indian frontier expeditions. I do not mean to infer that in the Chitral expedition there was not some firing into camp at night or attacks on isolated parties or individuals *after* the action of the Malakand, for this invariably happens, and may do so even after the representatives of the tribe have concluded terms of peace. Such attacks as those I refer to are often made by recalcitrant members of the tribe, who refuse to be bound by the decision or wishes of the majority, for no Pathan tribe owes permanent allegiance to any leader or leaders, though they often follow and obey some fanatical priest or leader with some special object in view, only to desert him at once if success is not obtained.

Such resistance as this, it was generally thought, might be expected, even after the Afridis and Orakzais had been worsted in one or more stand-up fights ; **but, so** far as **I** can remember, I never heard any officer, political **or** military, predict, nor **did** any Indian newspaper I read prophesy, that guerilla warfare of **the** most serious and organized nature would be carried on against our troops *after* the Sampagha and Arhanga passes **had** been carried and the main column was established in Tirah. Everything, on the contrary, seemed **to** point to the probability of both Orakzais and Afridis craving terms as soon as Tirah had been entered ; and people who now **say** and write that a serious and protracted campaign, with **almost** incessant resistance, might reasonably have **been** expected, have, **so far** as I am able to form an opinion, been wise after **the** event. There **was** another reason, **in** addition to the great moral effect **of** at once raising the unlifted **curtain, why** Tirah should be the first objective :—

viz., that as the operations only began late in the year, it was very important to visit the high-lying country of Tirah, with an average elevation in its valleys of about 6,000 feet, before the first fall of snow took place, which, besides entailing great sufferings on the troops and followers, might block the passes and render the movement of supplies and convoys very difficult. For these, and for probably many other reasons, the centre of Tirah was decided on as the first objective point to be aimed at in the campaign.

With this in view, Kohat was fixed as the base of operations for the troops of the main column, under Sir William Lockhart's direct command, whilst a force of about a brigade, termed the Peshawur column, under Brigadier-General Hammond, V.C., was formed at Peshawur, and another force, termed the Kurram column, under Brigadier-General Hill, was concentrated in the Kurram Valley. The composition of the main column, of the Peshawur and Kurram columns, and of the troops on the line of communication, under Sir Power Palmer, will be found in an appendix at the end of this book. Some slight alterations were afterwards made, both in the staff and in the distribution of the various units composing the brigades, &c.; but the table gives a fair idea of the composition of the force when it took the field.

A glance at the rough map of the country shows that, as the main column advanced into Tirah from Kohat, *viâ* Shinawari, it had the Kurram column on its left flank, and the Peshawur column on its right. This Peshawur column moved later on to Bara, and thence almost as far as Barkai on the Bara River, where it joined hands with the troops of the main column about the 14th of December. Early in October Sir William Lockhart issued from Kohat (through Sir Richard Udny, the chief political officer with the force) a manifesto to the various sections of the Orakzai and Afridi tribes, the general purport of which was that he had decided to enter Tirah and traverse the whole country; if no resistance to the advance of the troops were offered, no damage would be done to their towns, fortified houses, and property, and that the terms of the Indian Government would be made known to the tribesmen, who might send

Base and Lines of Communication.   55

in their jirgahs or deputations to hear them, when the force arrived in the centre of Tirah, and that till this point was reached no proposals from the tribesmen, for terms, would be listened to.

I shall now proceed to describe the base and lines of communication in so far as the main column is concerned.

Kohat may be reached in two ways from Peshawur. Firstly, by rail as far as Khusalgarh, and thence by metalled road, a distance of thirty-one miles. Secondly, by a very rough unmade track from Peshawur, which can be traversed in three marches. The last march, eighteen miles in length, passes through the Kohat Pass, which is not in British territory, but in the country of the Adam Khel tribe of Afridis. I have described this tribe in the first chapter, and explained how, owing to the excellent political relations existing between them and the political officer at Kohat, troops and transport animals were enabled to march from Peshawur to Kohat through the pass without molestation, and thus leave the branch railway line from near Rawal Pindi to Khusalgarh, and the road from thence into Kohat, free for the movement of troops and stores coming from other parts of India.

A light line of railway, laid from Khusalgarh *via* Kohat to Shinawari, would have immensely assisted the movement of stores, but the Indian Government has not as yet seen its way to afford the initial cost of such railways in India, though once established an enormous saving both in time and expense would be effected.

The principal means of transport between Khusalgarh and Kohat, and thence on to Shinawari, is by bullock-cart, a slow and tedious process. If, as was the case between Kohat and Shinawari, the line of communications is open to attack, the guarding of long trains of bullock-carts, many of which break down and block the road, becomes a difficult matter. The protection of a light railway, however, with its trains passing at stated times, would be comparatively easy.

The railway terminus at Khusalgarh is, as will be seen from the map, on the Indian side of the Indus River; and to cross the Indus two bridges of boats were constructed. But the approaches to these bridges were of such a difficult nature that, despite the fact that elephants were employed in helping to drag the heavily-laden bullock-carts up the steep portion of road, constant blocks and delays occurred at the bridges. The difficulty of the river-crossing could, however, only have been partially removed even if a light line of railway had been laid. An illustration of this boat-bridge over the Indus will be found facing page 46.

Writers who have held that Peshawur rather than Kohat should have been selected as the base of operations certainly have one strong argument in their favour, when they point out the difficulty of the river-crossing at Khusalgarh; for the Indus is bridged by the railway at Attock, between Rawal Pindi and Peshawur, and is therefore no hindrance to the movement of troops or stores. At the same time they overlook the very important fact, that although the line of communication round by Shinawari is a long one, it is nevertheless a good metalled road, fit for camels and wheeled traffic, also, that Karappa, one march on, was known, and that thence, in about three marches, the force would be in the heart of the Afridi Tirah. If, on the other hand, the advance had been made from Peshawur into Tirah, about sixty miles of absolutely unknown country would have to be traversed after leaving the Bara River, some twenty miles from Peshawur; thus, not only would it be impossible to use camel or wheeled transport, but the protection of the transport, moving possibly in deep gorges, along unmade and unknown tracks, would have been a most difficult matter.

To put the matter briefly: supposing Peshawur had been the base, and the Bara Valley route had been followed, in order to reach Bagh and Maidan (the same route, in fact, which Sir William Lockhart took when he marched from Bagh to Barkai in the Bara Valley early in December), the metalled portion of the line of communication would have been some fifteen miles long. Camels might have been used for another ten miles or so, but hence for about sixty miles nothing but mule, pony, and donkey transport would have been available, at any rate, until the road had been sufficiently widened and repaired to admit of camels using it.

With Kohat as the base, the metalled line of communications runs as far as Shinawari, and is about fifty miles in length. From Shinawari to Karappa, around which the country was known, is about twelve miles, while the centre of Maidan is distant another twenty miles. On the other hand, Kohat is thirty miles from the railway.

It will be seen, therefore, that the line of communications from Kohat, once the troops were assembled there, is very little longer. The greater portion of it lies along a metalled road running through very flat country, so that native cavalry could well be employed in moving along the line and protecting the convoys, a duty which is not only very fatiguing for infantry, but which cannot be so efficiently performed by them in open plain country.

The system of guarding the convoys, followed on the road between Kohat and Shinawari, was to start one off very early in the morning with a cavalry escort, whilst infantry pickets were posted on various hills and eminences commanding the road in order to deny their use to the enemy. These pickets were withdrawn at dusk, and no movement of transport animals or carts was permitted along the road after dark.

A few attacks were made on the transport, notably so on the 16th of October, when some eighteen bullock-carts belonging to a native contractor, the drivers of which, in defiance of all orders, had stopped on the road for the night to cook their food and sleep, were attacked by some raiders, who killed one driver and wounded five, and, having upset the carts, drove off the bullocks.

As long as the road is a metalled one, Government mule and bullock-carts, native contractors' bullock-carts, camels, and mule, pony, and donkey pack transport, can all be used on the same road. When it ceases to be metalled, and is rough, stony, and in bad condition, only mule, pony, and donkey transport can be taken. Camels can only use the road when it has undergone considerable improvement and widening.

Long before the railway train entered Khusalgarh station early in October, the tons of stores, compressed forage, tents, bags of grain, &c., piled at intervals for nearly a mile along each side of the railway, showed what vast preliminary measures are necessary for the concentration of a large force. From early morning till late at night the road from Khusalgarh to Kohat was covered by a constant stream of carts and animals going and returning, and by detachments of troops, British and native, marching along it. The block was especially great at the boat bridges over the Indus, about half a mile from the station at Khusalgarh.

A native driver, if he sees anything wrong with his bullocks or cart, never attempts to pull to one side of the road; he merely stops where he is, and proceeds very calmly and deliberately to try and repair the damage. It may be that, if one or two other natives would give a hand for a moment, when, for instance, a wheel has stuck in a rut, the difficulty would at once be got over; but no native driver in a case like this ever voluntarily assists another. The breakdown, meanwhile, of one cart, may be blocking two or three hundred others behind; and in most cases, if the driver of the cart causing the block would pull out of the road, or if two men standing by would afford him the least assistance, the difficulty would be at an end. But nothing of this sort ever happens unless considerable moral or even physical pressure is applied by the native or European overseer who chances to be on the spot.

Another difficulty is that no native driver ever pays any attention to the rule of the road. He goes to the right or left at his own sweet will, and quite regardless of the side to which the carts in front of him have gone. This is another fruitful source of delay, for carts coming the other way cannot pass. A bullock once brought to a halt frequently lies down, and requires immense persuasion to be induced to rise again; meanwhile the bullock-drivers further behind rather welcome the halt than otherwise, and having lighted their pipes, sit down to a comfortable chat and a smoke.

To be employed as a transport officer, with the charge of a road like the approach to the bridge over the Indus, where blocks occurred frequently, is one of the most exasperating things in creation. Every native, with his complete disregard of the value of time, is more or less annoying, but a bullock-driver especially so. I have seen a young member of the Indian Civil Service, fresh from the University, and full of ideas as to the regeneration of India and the evils resulting from the too peremptory measures employed in dealing with the down-trodden native, descend from his pony-cart and cuff with the greatest zest and vigour the head of a bullock-driver who had drawn his bullock-cart right across the road, and was philosophically smoking his pipe, regardless of all other people who wanted to pass.

When I ventured to remark that his peremptory measures were not in accordance with his formerly freely expressed views as to the *suaviter in modo* being the only right way to deal with a native, he remarked that "circumstances alter cases." But whereas with him the temptation to wrath arose but once, with a transport officer it occurs daily, hourly, and every five minutes.

When, with the help of elephants, the bullock carts, after crossing the bridge, had been again drawn up on to level ground things went a little better. But the whole way to Shinawari, small if not wholesale blocks occurred, and far away, as one looked forward or backward, a thick cloud of dust hung above the road, pointing out its direction clearly, even when cuttings or undulations of the ground concealed the animals moving on it.

Kohat, the point for which all the laden transport from Khusalgarh was making, was in like manner indicated by the cloud of dust and smoke which hung over it, long before the houses in the cantonment itself could be seen. As one approached it seemed to be surrounded by an absolute sea of canvas. Regiments, batteries, and hospitals, were encamped wherever there was a vacant space, under every tree which afforded any shade, and in the garden or enclosure of every house. Practically, wherever there was the least level space, a little tent, with a *tente d'abri* in most cases behind it, could be seen, indicating where an officer and his native servant were living.

The houses themselves, and even the verandas, were in most cases crammed with officers—two, three, or even four in a room—and the roads of the cantonment were crowded with every form of transport animals. This was still more the case after the 12th of October, for, from that date on, columns of troops marched in almost daily from Peshawur *viâ* the Kohat Pass;

THE COMMISSARIAT DEPÔT, KOHAT.

[*To face page* 64.

the first of these columns being commanded by Brigadier-General Ian Hamilton, and the distance covered in the last march being about eighteen miles.

The troops, which consisted of about four regiments, were accompanied by 1,300 camels and 600 mules; and their march was accomplished without any fighting, for the Afridis of the Kohat Pass were friendly disposed. Nevertheless, the road was of so stony and rough a nature, and the narrow route became so encumbered with transport, that although a start was made at 4.30 A.M., it was fully 8 o'clock in the evening before the rearguard succeeded in getting into camp. Brigadier-General Ian Hamilton had the misfortune to break his leg soon after, and was succeeded in command of the first brigade by Brigadier-General Hart, V.C.

Under normal circumstances Kohat is a quiet and compact little cantonment with about three regiments, all belonging to the Panjaub Frontier Force, as its garrison; but in the month of October, 1897, it was swollen to such an extent by the stores, troops, and transport animals that anyone who had seen it in its former condition would have almost failed to recognise it from a distance. The whole line of communication was under the command of Lieutenant-General Sir Power Palmer, with a numerous staff to assist him; and his command included the whole length of road from Khusalgarh to Shinawari. This line of communication was divided up into sections, each of which had a staff officer solely responsible, as commandant, for all the road and the posts or depôts in his section.

The work of such officers is never-ceasing; not only have they to take precautions for defending each depôt or post, but convoys have to be forwarded and escorted, the condition of the road looked to and reported on, and dead animals buried.

From the 10th to the 20th October one continuous stream of troops and transport animals moved along the road, sometimes as many as 2,000 carts alone leaving one post for the next; and if viewed from an eminence, there did not appear to be a space of more than fifty yards, anywhere, that was not occupied by troops, transport animals, or bullock-carts.

The commissariat officers at Khusalgarh and Kohat were working day and night in unloading, issuing, and arranging stores for onward dispatch; and upon them, and the transport officers, fell the main work of preparing for the advance of the army.

In the next chapter I shall deal with the difficulties which the transport officers had to contend with, and which, despite all the efforts they made, could not be entirely surmounted.

CHAPTER IV.

THE TRANSPORT.

In all armies the question of the transport, or the means of conveying the necessary stores, ammunition, and various impedimenta is a matter of the utmost importance, for on it depends in a very large measure the mobility of the army in the field. No European nation maintains on a war footing either all the men or all the transport which will be required in time of war; and whereas the number of men is made up from those who have already been trained and passed to the reserve, the complement of animals and carts is obtained by impressing horses and vehicles, the property of private companies and individuals, into the public service.

Until comparatively recent times the value of the magnificent force of volunteers, which we possess in England, was largely discounted by the fact that if they were to take the field the Government would not be able to provide them with sufficient transport to enable them to move; and the same remark applied equally to the Militia.

The difficulty of providing transport for the Home Army, in the event of mobilization, has now been to a very large extent overcome by paying a fixed yearly sum to the owners of suitable horses and vehicles; and in return for this subsidy, these owners agree to let the Government take over from them, when a force is mobilized, the animals and carts required. In this way the military authorities in England, without being put to the expense of maintaining transport that would be far in excess of peace requirements, have nevertheless a lien on a sufficient quantity to suit their purpose whenever the need may arise.

Great as are the difficulties in England and, generally speaking, throughout Europe in connection with transport, it must be remembered that these countries are not so handicapped as India, possessing as they do a network of railways and metalled roads. One railway train alone can carry an amount of stores that would require several thousand camels, and still more mules, ponies, or donkeys, to transport; and in Europe, pack transport need only in isolated instances be resorted to.

In some of the operations in Burma, the river Irrawaddy was very largely used for transport as far as the lines of communications were concerned; but in all operations on the north-west frontier of India, even the base can seldom be on a line of railway, and wheeled transport can of course only be used where there are good metalled roads. As soon, therefore, as troops enter the country where active operations are to begin, nothing but pack transport can be resorted to; and in all probability some considerable time must elapse before the tracks used in the first instance by mule, pony, and donkey transport can be made passable for laden camels, the carrying capacity of which largely exceeds that of mules.

It is only when a comparatively small force takes the field that the Indian Government can equip it with what is termed "Government transport." The camels have invariably to be bought or hired, and, as the number of mules in India—which are far and away the best and hardiest pack animals—is comparatively limited, the necessary complement has to be made up by buying or hiring ponies and donkeys—both unsatisfactory animals for transport purposes, and liable to die in large numbers.

At the time the Tirah Expedition was formed, some other expeditions were only just over, and in two instances the troops had been maintained on a war footing near the scene of operations—that is, in the Tochi Valley and on the Malakand Pass. A very large amount of transport animals was therefore required, and the following table shows better than any description the immense quantity of beasts which such expeditions absorb where there are no railways and but few metalled roads.

Force to which attached.	Camels and Bullocks.	Other Pack Animals.
Tirah Expedition	13,370	29,440
Peshawur Column	980	3,220
Kurram Valley	2,390	280
Rawal Pindi Reserve Brigade	670	460
Malakand Field Force	3,320	2,950
Tochi Force	4,200	2,300
Kohat Garrison	750	180
Peshawur Garrison	790	500
Reserve Animals	3,000	3,000
	29,470	42,330

This makes a grand total of nearly seventy-two thousand animals, of which all but about thirteen thousand were required in connection with the campaign against the Orakzais and the Afridis; and as out of this large number only a comparatively small proportion were Government animals, the surplus required had to be bought or hired.

I think it **was** admitted on all sides that the resources of Northern India were not equal to the demand, and the transport animals, more particularly the ponies and donkeys with which some of the troops **were** provided, were absolutely unfit **for the** purpose in view.

Whether this **was** due to the strain caused by **the** previous expeditions, and to the enormous number **of animals** required **for the Tirah** expedition, or **whether** it was that the officers deputed to assist **the** commissariat officers in buying the necessary animals **were too** young and inexperienced, it is **hard to** say. But **the** fact remains that a very **large proportion of** those which were bought and sent to Kohat, more especially the ponies, were **obviously** quite useless **for** the purpose, **being** narrow-chested **and** hocked, and hardly **able to** carry more than the comparatively heavy ordnance saddles with which they were equipped.

There are now in India a large number of Imperial Service Troops, entirely paid, equipped and maintained by the loyal native princes of India, and placed by them at the disposal of Government in case their services are required.

Most of these troops consist of cavalry and infantry; and representatives of the officers amongst the Imperial Service cavalry, conspicuous amongst them Sir Pertab Singh, figured in the last Jubilee procession. Some of the native princes of India, however, either in addition to or in the place of cavalry and infantry regiments, maintain a company of engineers—or sappers and miners as they are termed in India—whilst the rulers of Jeypore and Gwalior each keep up an admirably equipped transport train.

The animals in these transport trains consist entirely of ponies, strong well-bred animals, all trained to pack-saddle work, to go in harness, and to drag the little pony transport carts with which the train is equipped. Their pack-saddles are adjustable, and can be used either in harness or simply and solely as pack-saddles, whilst the drivers are properly trained and enlisted soldiers. Moreover, instead of one man having charge of three pack animals, as is the case with Government transport, one man is told off to every two ponies, so that not only can the animals be better fed, groomed, and looked after in the lines, but there is much less fear of loads slipping, or animals getting sore backs, or giving trouble in other ways on the march. These Jeypore and Gwalior transport trains, placed as they were entirely at the service of the Indian Government, were of the greatest possible assistance; and their animals showed a marked contrast to the ponies bought and hired just before the Tirah Expedition. Not only was much of the delay at the beginning of the campaign due (to use a very mild term) to the inferior transport, but a great many of the animals bought for the expedition, instead of being sent to Kohat ready equipped, were dispatched without pack-saddles, bridles, or any equipment at all. The transport officers, whose hands were already quite full with apportioning out the required number of animals to the different regiments and units, had also to busy themselves in providing the numerous newly-bought and under-sized ponies with pack-saddles and equipment. As a result of the extra and incessant work thus thrown on their shoulders, no time was available to brand the animals and apportion them out for use to corps in such a way as to ensure any that strayed being easily recognised.

Wherever there is a large military camp with many thousand animals, it must always happen that some of them get loose and wander. If, however, they have been branded in such a way that the corps to which they belong can be easily ascertained, all loose and stray animals can be taken back to their proper lines, and steps taken to find out the person or persons responsible for their being at large. Some native drivers undoubtedly allowed weakly animals in their charge to stray away, in the hope that they might get better ones in their place ; but most of the animals, no doubt, got loose because they had been carelessly secured. At every camp there were large numbers of such wanderers ; they would stray away, roll, and get rid of their clothing, and, having failed to get their evening feed, would be found in the early morning dead or dying of the cold. At the camp at Bagh, during the end of November and the beginning of December, when there were fifteen degrees of frost and more every night, the stray ponies and donkeys died in great numbers; and though steps were taken to collect and feed all such animals, their numbers would have been far fewer, and consequently the losses by cold and starvation much less, if it had been possible to identify them, and thus ascertain who was in fault.

It is a great question whether the use of the comparatively cheap pony and donkey, instead of the more expensive mule, is not a penny-wise and pound-foolish policy, for the mortality among the former animals was very great. The mules, however, were the only animals that withstood the rigorous cold in Maidan and Tirah.

A pony cannot ordinarily carry the same load as a mule, much less a donkey; and they are both more liable to sore backs, and less able to resist the cold. Although, after the experiences of the Afghan War, it was reported that the transport authorities in India had resolved that camels and mules would, in future expeditions, be the only animals employed for pack transport with the force, time has gone on, and ponies and donkeys have again had to be resorted to; the Government of India having apparently been unwilling to undergo the expense of providing a sufficient number of mules for all requirements.

In discussing the quality of the transport animals provided at the beginning of the Tirah Expedition, I have spoken principally of the pack-animals intended to accompany the force in the field; but in addition to these there were of course a very large number of camels and bullocks, working simply and solely on the metalled line of communication between Khusalgarh and Shinawari.

There were various methods of transporting stores between these two places, in so far as their conveyance by wheeled carriage was concerned, the principal vehicle being of course the bullock-cart. Those employed were of three descriptions, viz., "hired contractors' carts," "maundagi carts," and "Government carts." The first-mentioned are those hired from contractors or private individuals at so much a day, including the driver; and the carts are made to carry what is considered a fair load according to commissariat and transport regulations. This system works fairly. When regiments are on the march in India, the bulk of the baggage is generally conveyed in carts of this description; though sometimes camel transport is supplied. But its great objection, either in peace or war, is the fact that the drivers, who are frequently, if not generally, the owners of the bullocks and carts, are in many cases hiring them out to Government most unwillingly.

To people who have not been in the East, it may appear a very simple matter to employ only those native bullock-drivers who are really anxious to let out their carts for hire. It would, however, be quite impossible for the Indian Government to deal directly with individuals, for these drivers are devoid of education, and I might even add of intelligence. The system of middlemen or intermediaries is such a part and parcel of the Oriental character and customs, that few, if any, transactions take place between a white man and the *executive* Oriental—by which term I mean to imply the man who will actually execute the desired work—without the intervention of one or more *administrative* natives, each of whom will exact a greater or less commission from the man who actually does the work. If, therefore, a certain number of hired carts are wanted on Government service from a particular district, the military authorities acquaint the civil authorities, who in turn inform the Deputy Commissioner or Civil Administrator of the district. He in turn applies to the native magistrates or tehsildars under him, each of whom has charge of a portion of the district. The tehsildar informs the head men of certain villages, and sooner than offend the all-powerful tehsildar, the drivers, carts, and bullocks are produced, though very frequently the drivers are in reality most averse to leaving their homes. This reluctance is generally not so much due to the nature of the work they are wanted for, as to the fact that the drivers or actual owners of the carts seldom or never receive more than a moiety of the very fair remuneration which the Government of India pays for each cart.

Every native official, the tehsildar included, expects a commission on each cart he has helped to supply, so that by the time each *administrative* native has received his share, comparatively little remains for the *executive* native, or bullock-driver, who has alone borne all the burden and heat of the day. It might be urged that if a rule were made that the drivers of the carts should be paid directly by a British officer, they would in that case get the whole sum due to them. This is far from being the case. Pressure would at once be exercised to make them pay up the commission to the people who expected it; and in nine cases out of ten they would voluntarily part with a percentage of their wages, for a native regards the tyranny to which he is subjected by his richer brethren as a matter of course.

No amount of Acts of Parliament or Orders in Council can even modify to any great extent, much less change, this system; it is far too deeply ingrained in the Oriental character. In fact there is no public and hardly any private transaction, in which money changes hands, without one or more people levying a commission from it.

In the case of famine relief works or gangs of coolies working on a railway, it is almost sure to happen either that the labourers pay back a percentage of their wages to the native overseer, or if not, that the latter individual draws pay for many more men than are actually employed; when a muster or count-over of the workmen is made, he calls in outside men so as to temporarily make up the number. If a private individual buys any article whatsoever from a native merchant who comes to his house, the head servant in the household is certain to receive back a percentage. And if a person were to send for eight or ten coolies or native porters to carry his baggage on a march, each of the coolies would pay a percentage on his small earnings to the village head man, or, if hired in a cantonment, to the native contractor.

Whenever Government or private individuals employ native labour, they are bound to make use of native intermediaries to collect the workmen; and not only does the coolie in many cases give his services unwillingly, but he seldom or never pockets the full sum due to him—not even if you pay him the money yourself into his own hand and see him off the premises. Some one, either one of your servants or a native contractor, is sure to exact a commission; and the word *dasturi*—the Hindustani equivalent for commission — means "what is customary,"—no small proof in itself of how deep-rooted the system is.

I have dwelt on this subject at some length, because I have seen remarks in various newspapers that a large proportion of the drivers and native followers had to serve against their will; and while quite admitting it is the case, I have endeavoured to show that it is in a great measure due to this system of commission—a system which, after all, in some of its forms, is not entirely unknown in England.

To return to the native contractors' carts. The drivers of these are, in many cases, engaged against their will, and to avoid serving frequently pretend that they are ill, or that their bullocks cannot drag the loads; or they will tamper with their carts to make them break down, or under-feed the bullocks. This is the main drawback to "hired contractors' carts."

The next system of transport is that of "maundagi carts." A "maund" is about eighty-two pounds, or half a mule load, and the term "maundagi carts" means that a native contractor is paid so much per maund safely delivered at its destination. The great disadvantage of this system is that the carts are constantly overloaded, for the native contractor naturally tries to carry the maximum load at the minimum cost, and breakdowns constantly occur. Such mishaps not only block the road for the remainder of the transport, but entail great difficulties in the way of protecting the broken-down carts if the driver and bullocks cannot be got into camp by nightfall.

The third system of conveyance in carts is by Government mule or bullock-cart. In this expedition the Jeypore and the Gwalior transport trains, that is the light carts with a pair of ponies in each, together with the Indian Government mule and bullock-carts, were also used in working along the metalled road to Shinawari.

All the Government wheeled transport, together with the Jeypore and Gwalior carts, worked admirably, and if only the hired contractors' carts and the "maundagi" carts could have been dispensed with, the constant blocks, breakdowns, and delays on the road would have been almost entirely obviated. The expense of maintaining, in time of peace, sufficient wheeled transport to work a long line of communication for a large force is probably almost prohibitive. But if the plant and rolling-stock of a light railway were kept in store at one or more convenient places on the frontier, the comparatively small initial expense would very soon be more than repaid, for a considerable saving would be effected by reducing the number of bullock-carts, drivers, etc., which would otherwise have to be maintained or hired.

The advantages which even a light railway possesses in comparison with wheeled traffic by road are enormous. Once the line has been laid there is comparatively little wear and tear of the permanent way, whereas a road requires incessant mending, particularly in country where there is often a deficiency of water to enable the metalling to "bind" well. The transport of the sick and wounded can also be effected rapidly, and with the minimum of discomfort to the patients; whilst the road, if it runs parallel to the railway, can be utilised for marching troops and for subsidiary transport purposes. Heavy stores, such as ammunition, which are difficult to move in carts, can also be easily and quickly transported by rail, and there is no such thing as straggling carts and animals, which cannot keep up with the remainder of the convoy.

It is, moreover, very difficult for an enemy, especially when he is unprovided with the necessary explosives for demolition purposes, to effectually damage or block a railway. If rails are removed they can be replaced without difficulty, except at curves; whilst all vulnerable points, such as bridges under a railway, the destruction of which might block the line for several days, can easily have special guards assigned to them. Instead of a constant stream of carts, the trains would run at fixed times and could carry with them a small escort, and the difficulty of escorting the convoy and guarding the line along its entire length would be greatly lessened.

If a British force ever requires to advance from Quetta to Kandahar, all the plant for extending the railway line in that direction is stored ready for use at the terminus. The material for a light railway could with great facility be moved from one or more central depôts to wherever it was required; though it must be admitted that as regards Khusalgarh, the fact of the Indus not being bridged, would have necessitated the railway plant being taken for about half a mile in bullock carts till the river was crossed ; but even so, the saving in time and money would have been immense.

Once, however, a point has been reached beyond which no metalled road has been made, recourse must invariably be had to pack transport. And it is to be hoped that the Indian Government may see its way eventually to largely increase the stock of mules, so that the use of ponies and donkeys may be absolutely dispensed with in future campaigns. Needless to say, the commissariat and transport officers did the very best they could with the transport at their disposal, a large percentage of which, they were only too ready to admit, was quite unfit for the purpose required ; but the movements of the main column were undoubtedly much hampered by the indifferent transport right up to the time the force moved from Maidan to Bagh, towards the end of November. After that date arrangements were made for sending back as many of the unserviceable transport ponies and donkeys as had not already succumbed, to the base and to the line of communications, and for replacing them by mules and strong ponies. So, when the first and second divisions moved from Tirah into the Bara Valley, the whole of the transport animals were well suited for the difficult marches which lay before them.

CHAPTER V.

ENGLISH AS COMPARED WITH INDIAN ARMY ORGANIZATIONS, AND EUROPEAN AS COMPARED WITH SAVAGE WARFARE.

The composition of a force for field service in India varies in many essential particulars from that which obtains on the Continent or in England. The main difference is, that whereas in the latter country the composition of an army is by Army Corps, in India there is no such tactical organization, the largest unit being a division.

In the English, as distinguished from the Indian Army, the Army Corps consist of three divisions, of two brigades each; and in addition to this there are a certain number of what are termed "corps troops." A brigade consists of four regiments of infantry, a field company Royal Engineers, and one company Army Service Corps. The division, in addition to these two brigades, has a squadron of cavalry and three batteries of field artillery. The

Army Corps, in addition to the three divisions, which comprise between them twenty-four regiments of infantry, three squadrons of cavalry, and nine batteries of artillery, has for "corps troops" one regiment of infantry, one squadron of cavalry, from five to eight batteries of artillery (termed the "corps artillery"), and various engineer units, such as a field park, a balloon section, a pontoon train, some field telegraph companies, and some more Army Service Corps details. There are, of course, field hospitals, bearer companies, ammunition columns, etc., besides; but it is to the strictly combatant portions of an Army Corps that I wish to draw attention.

It will be noticed that whereas there are twenty-five regiments of infantry and from fourteen to seventeen batteries of artillery, there are only four squadrons, or one regiment of cavalry, in a whole Army Corps. The reason of this is that the squadron of cavalry attached to the division is what is known as "divisional cavalry;" and in all probability a cavalry division (some six regiments of cavalry, two batteries Horse Artillery, a battalion of mounted infantry, and a mounted detachment

Royal Engineers) will take the field and act in conjunction with the army in the field, which may consist of one or more Army Corps.

In the war of 1870 the Germans took the field with three armies, each consisting of three or more Army Corps; and the composition of an Army Corps on the Continent is almost identical with that in England, except that the English is, as far as I know, the only one in which the Army Corps consists of three divisions. In continental armies there are only two divisions, but these are as a rule considerably stronger than our divisions in the proportion of cavalry and artillery.

The Indian Army is organised for field service by brigades and divisions; and "Divisional Troops," in a division, take the place of "Corps Troops" in the Army Corps. The brigade consists of four regiments of infantry, two British and two native, and a hospital establishment; the division consists of two brigades, and has, as a general rule, for its divisional troops, one regiment of native cavalry, three batteries of artillery, a regiment of native infantry (pioneers, as a rule), and a company of engineers or sappers and miners, with a hospital establishment in addition.

If one or more of these divisions is working in country suitable for the action of cavalry, there will probably be also a cavalry brigade working in advance of the division or divisions in the same way as the cavalry division works ahead of one or more Army Corps.

There are without doubt many good reasons why an organisation by Army Corps has not been thought suitable in India. In the first place, the important fact must be remembered that in England or on the Continent an Army Corps could move with its three divisions on roads more or less parallel to one another, and, as it is termed, within "touching distance;" so close, that is to say, that communication between them could be easily maintained and all three could combine for attack or defence. In India, on the other hand, and more especially beyond its borders, no such network of roads exists; and it could rarely happen that the roads or tracks, or even the country itself (if an army was moving off roads), would lend themselves to the movement of three divisions in parallel lines in such a way that the Army Corps Commander could exercise a control and supervision over all his divisions. So much so is this the case, that during the Tirah campaign it was argued by some writers, and with a show of reason, that even an organisation by divisions is cumbrous for mountain warfare. If the highest unit had been a brigade, with a proportion of artillery and sappers and miners attached, the force would have been more mobile; and it could have worked with a smaller staff than when organised as it was in divisions, because each division had its own general and staff in addition to the brigadier-general and staff with each brigade.

The detailed composition of each brigade and division will be found in an appendix at the end of the book, and I propose in this chapter to give only a very brief resumé of the composition of the force.

General Sir William Lockhart, K.C.B., K.C.S.I., was given the command of the whole force. Few officers have had more experience than he of active service, more especially on the frontier; and he had as Chief of the Staff, Brigadier-General Nicholson, C.B., the Deputy Adjutant-General of the Punjaub

Army, who has also seen much frontier service. The main column, which was to operate from Kohat, consisted of the first and second divisions, each of two brigades. Major-General Symons, C.B., commanded the first division, whilst Brigadier-General Ian Hamilton, C.B., D.S.O., commanded the 1st Brigade, till he had the misfortune to break his leg early in October, and was succeeded by Brigadier-General Hart, C.B., V.C. Brigadier-General Gaselee, C.B., A.D.C., commanded the 2nd Brigade.

The second division contained the 3rd and 4th Brigades, and was commanded by Major-General Yeatman-Biggs, C.B., who died at Peshawur, soon after the march down the Bara Valley was over, from the effects of the constant campaigning he had undergone. Brigadier-General Kempster, D.S.O., A.D.C., commanded the 3rd Brigade, and Brigadier-General Westmacott, C.B., D.S.O., the 4th Brigade.

Lieutenant-General Sir Power Palmer, K.C.B., was in command of the lines of communication, extending from Khusalgarh to the most advanced depôt. Brigadier-General Hammond, C.B., D.S.O., V.C., A.D.C., commanded the Peshawur column and Colonel Hill, Colonel on the Staff, commanded the Kurram movable column, while the Reserve Brigade at Rawal Pindi was commanded by Brigadier-General Macgregor, D.S.O.

The total nominal strength of the force was as follows :—

British officers	1,010
British rank and file	10,822
Native officers and men	22,614
Native followers	19,858
Horses	4,328
Ponies	5,231
Mules	14,623
Bullocks	160

The above details of transport animals do not include those required for the carriage of supplies, but only those necessary for accompanying the troops; the total number of animals employed on or in connection with the Tirah expedition being, in round numbers, 41,000, or taking reserve animals into consideration, about 45,000.

Sir Richard Udny, the Indian Civil Service Commissioner of Peshawur, was chief political officer of the force, and, to assist him in dealing with the Afridis, he had Colonel Warburton, who was for many years political officer in the Khyber Pass.

I have noted, at the beginning of this chapter, some of the main differences between the English and the Indian army organisation, and I now propose to touch very briefly on some of the main points of difference between European or civilized warfare, where two civilized armies come into collision, and savage, or, as it would perhaps better be described, non-European warfare.

Whereas the principles of conducting European warfare vary only in some degree with the nature of the country in which the hostile forces meet, the principles of non-European warfare,—in which I include warlike operations against a semi-civilized or a savage foe,—differ very widely indeed, according to the character of the enemy, the nature of the country, and more particularly the method of fighting adopted by the inhabitants of the country either amongst themselves or against an invader.

In European warfare, as waged under normal conditions, the tactical dispositions would generally aim at employing a large force of cavalry to move in front of the army, with the object of screening and covering the strength and movements of the force behind it, and at the same time endeavouring, by pushing back the hostile cavalry, to ascertain the enemy's numbers and dispositions. Once the enemy has been found in position and prepared to oppose any further forward movement, the attacking force, using the cavalry for protecting its flanks, for hostile operations against the enemy's flanks, and possibly even against his line of retreat, brings every available gun into action with the view of silencing the hostile batteries. It then directs the bulk of its artillery fire against one or more of the points in the enemy's line which it is intended to assault.

When it is considered that they have been sufficiently shaken by artillery fire, the infantry as a rule advances to the assault in three lines, being especially strong opposite the point where the attack has to be driven home. Opposite other portions of the enemy's line the *rôle* of the infantry will probably be to fight what is termed a demonstrative action, by pretending to assault and by bringing such a heavy fire to bear on the troops in front of it, that the opposing general may not be able to move his reserves to the real point of attack. Facing the real point or points of assault the attacking infantry force endeavours to penetrate like a wedge into the enemy's line, and, with this object in view, brings every rifle for which there is room into the first line. The second line, which is of great strength, backs up the first line, and, in conjunction with it, forces its way into the position; whilst a very strong third line, or general reserve, follows up behind the second with the main view of meeting a counter attack or covering a retreat. If the position is taken, the object is to prevent recapture, and join the cavalry and artillery prosecuting the pursuit.

On the defensive, the cavalry has very much the same *rôle* as that of the cavalry of the army taking the offensive, viz., to obtain information and, as far as possible, prevent the hostile cavalry from obtaining any. A position having been selected from which it is intended to bar the enemy's advance and offer battle, the defending infantry is formed as a rule in three lines. The first, consisting, as in the attack, of firing line, with supports and reserves, occupies the front of the position, lightly in places where the ground is naturally strong, and in greater force where it is not so, or where it seems to offer greater facilities for assault. The second line is generally posted so as to protect the flanks and reinforce the troops in the first line. The third line, or general reserve, has the very important *rôle* of rapidly moving to the point where it is seen the main attack is going to be delivered, of covering a retreat, and, most important of all, if the general is acting on the offensive-defensive of assuming the offensive when the enemy has exhausted himself in the attack, and of delivering a counter attack when the opportune moment is deemed to have arrived.

The artillery of the defending army is posted from the beginning of the action so as to command important roads and approaches, or to take assaulting columns in flank. If it is likely to be overwhelmed by the preponderating force of hostile artillery, it may possibly be temporarily withdrawn from action; but in any case, when the hostile infantry has approached a point within decisive range, the guns both of the defending and attacking forces will, in a very large measure, turn all their attention on the opposing infantry, for, in the case of the attack, the latter is the only arm by which the actual assault can be delivered, whilst in the case of the defence, it is the arm which, if defeated and driven back, must, sooner or later, carry with it both its cavalry and artillery.

Whether the army is acting on the offensive or defensive, it is sure to depend for its supplies, both of food and ammunition, on a line of communications. Provided an army is advancing, or is posted on the front of, at right angles with, or nearly so to its line of communications so as to cover it, that line is tolerably secure, except against a cavalry raid or the attacks of hostile inhabitants, both of which can be guarded against by comparatively small protecting forces. If an army, therefore, is not "forming front to a flank," but is covering its line of communications or retreat by advancing, or by being posted on a front, at right angles to it, or nearly so, that line can only be seriously threatened by the opposing force making a wide *détour* in order to attack it. But a force attempting to adopt such a measure would expose its own line of communications or retreat; and all the history of war tends to show that where two opponents are endeavouring to threaten each other's line of communications, that army whose line is first threatened must give way and fall back to cover it.

For the same reason, when two European armies are operating one against the other, and each is covering its own line of communications and of retreat, instead of forming front to a flank (*i.e.*, parallel to the line of retreat), not only is the line secure, but so also is the rear of each force; an army halted has therefore only to cover its front and flanks with its outposts.

Non-European warfare differs, in many respects, from that which I have described above, and in no way more than in regard to the protection of the line of communication.

I will now deal very briefly with some of the main points in which all savage, or non-European warfare, differs from that of civilized people. Few non-civilized nations possess ordnance, and, therefore, one's own artillery can come into action at much shorter ranges than would otherwise be the case; and there is not the same necessity for massing or concentrating the guns.

No savage nation, as far as I am aware, employs second and third lines of troops, either in the attack or the defence, and consequently, if the first line —which contains every available man—is defeated, the enemy has no general reserve to bring up to cover his retreat or make a counter attack. Once such a foe has been defeated no rearguard is formed to cover a retreat, and the loss of *morale* is infinitely greater than in a European force.

In attacking an Asiatic foe in position, a flank attack may be separated from a frontal attack to a much greater extent than would be safe in European warfare. In the former case the enemy never has either the reserve of troops in hand, nor the generalship to contain or hold back one attack with a comparatively small force, and fall in overwhelming strength on the other; as Napoleon did at Austerlitz, and Wellington at Salamanca.

Lastly, on account of the advantages which civilized troops possess over savage or semi-barbarous foes, owing to the power of discipline and of better weapons, and to the possession of artillery and machine-guns, a well-handled European force can resist or attack with every chance of success a much greater force of savages or semi-barbarians than it could of disciplined Europeans.

These appear the main respects in which a European force has the advantage over a savage or semi-barbarous force, though, doubtless, many other points of superiority will readily suggest themselves to the reader.

It is, however, rather to those matters in which we are at a disadvantage in dealing with a savage foe that I wish to draw attention, more particularly because some of the writers who have so freely criticised the campaign in Tirah appear to have lost sight of them.

The Soudanese warrior as he existed in the days of El Teb and Tamai, the Ghazi fanatic we have so often encountered on the North-Western frontier of India, and the Zulu of Ulundi, are individuals for whom death had no terrors at all, and who, regardless of losses amongst their comrades and their own wounds, charged recklessly home. In the Soudan and in the Zulu campaign our forces were fighting a nation of individuals of this character.

On the frontier the Ghazi has formed only a percentage of the opposing force; and with the remainder of the tribe, valour is generally, as with Europeans, mingled with discretion.

But when excited by the prowess of their Ghazi brethren, or elated by success, they are resolute and bold; and if hopeful of victory, or when temporarily excited by a fanatical preacher to expect a safe conduct to Paradise in case of death, their daring and courage is of the most reckless description.

A frontier tribesman can live for days on the grain he carries with him, and other savages on a few dates; consequently no necessity exists for them to cover a line of communications. So nimble of foot, too, are they in their grass shoes, and so conversant with every goat-track in their mountains, that they can retreat in any direction. This extraordinary mobility enables them to attack from any direction quite unexpectedly, and to disperse and disappear as rapidly as they came. For this reason the rear of a European force is as much exposed to attack as its front or flanks; and as the line of communications can be cut at almost any point, not only have the various depôts on the line of communications to be very strongly fortified, but all convoys moving along the road must be well guarded, and hills commanding the road held by pickets.

Troops or convoys moving in the dusk render themselves liable to annihilation, for a savage foe can see in the dark far better than a European, can approach noiselessly unseen, and attack simultaneously from all sides.

Whereas some savages are so inexperienced in the use of firearms, and so reckless that they prefer to trust to shock tactics and to their spears, the Pathan, and more especially the Afridi, is as skilled a marksman as could be found in the world. His rifle is to him the joy of his life. He has been brought up to use firearms from boyhood; and has probably been engaged from early manhood in trying to shoot one or more kinsmen or fellow-tribesmen with whom he has a blood feud. Frequently he has served in the Indian Army and learnt all that a musketry instructor can teach him; so that, when our troops are halted or in camp, he has a target to fire at which he can hardly miss. On the other hand, his dirty garments are so indistinguishable from the surrounding rocks, and he moves about with such agility, that he is comparatively safe.

So great again is his ferocity and his love for bloodshed that, with two or three comrades, he will lie concealed for hours in the hope of cutting up and mutilating some unarmed straggler or follower, or, better still, shooting some armed man and possessing himself of a rifle which is worth its weight in silver. So little does he think of the future that the loss of his house, his store of grain, and his fodder, is as nothing to the young Afridi, when compared with the present delight of murder and plunder; and he well knows that, were his tribe to combine and meet us in open fight, our discipline and armament would prevail, whereas his guerilla tactics offer him personally the maximum chance of plunder and success with the minimum of risk.

Such is the enemy we had to deal with in Tirah; a nation of skilled marksmen, masters of guerilla warfare, amply provided with arms and ammunition, fleet of foot as goats, and inhabiting a country as difficult as any in the world. No wonder is it if our losses have been severe in comparison with what we inflicted on them in return. The troops we can oppose to such foes are, with the exception of the Ghoorkhas, far less accustomed to hill-climbing than the Pathan; they are encumbered by boots, they have ammunition, and they possibly carry a great coat and a day's cooked rations. The Pathan, on the other hand, having stored his spare ammunition and food in some convenient hiding-place or in a spot that is inaccessible for our troops, goes forth to the fray far more lightly equipped even than the Ghoorkha scouts, who are specially trained and equipped for rapid movement in the hills.

In European warfare a dead or a wounded man can be left where he is, with the certainty that the enemy will bury the former and humanely treat the latter; in frontier warfare, the dead, and much more the wounded, have to be carried away; otherwise, the former would be desecrated and the latter tortured, mutilated, and killed, if they were to fall into a Pathan's hands. This removal of the dead and wounded while under close fire is one of the most difficult things in Pathan warfare, for it takes probably four men to carry a wounded comrade and another man to carry the five rifles. This knot of men offers a mark to the Afridi, of which he never fails to avail himself; and in this way one wounded man begets another. Even the graves of men who have fallen have to be concealed as far as possible, for an Afridi will not hesitate to disinter a corpse and wreak his vengeance by mutilating the body.

Though, of course, we have killed far fewer of them than would have been the case had they opposed us in stand-up fights, still the damage we have done them in consumption of fodder and grain, and in the destruction of their fortified houses and towns has been incalculable. These factors will doubtless be taken into account when the voices of the greybeards make themselves heard above those of the young hot-bloods, and they consider the question of giving in to the terms of the Indian Government or indefinitely continuing the war.

CHAPTER VI.

THE PREPARATIONS FOR THE ADVANCE AND THE FIRST ACTION OF DARGAI.

NEARLY the whole of September, 1897, had been spent by the Commissariat and Transport Departments in collecting huge stores of supplies at Khusalgarh and Kohat; and towards the end of September and the early part of October these began to be pushed forward to the advanced depôt at Shinawari, which is four marches from Kohat.

Meanwhile the troops which were to form the main column of the expeditionary force began to pour into Kohat. Some came from Khusalgarh, having arrived by rail from different parts of India, others from Peshawur, marching through the Kohat Pass, which runs through the territory of a friendly, or at all events neutral, tribe of the Afridis, who receive a yearly subsidy from the Indian Government for giving us the "right of way." As these

troops arrived they were gradually pushed on to Shinawari, the object being to concentrate there, first the remainder of the second division, and then the first division.

Some troops of the second—Major-General Yeatman-Biggs's—division were already on the spot, having taken part in the operations he had conducted on and about the Samana range at the end of August and through a great part of September; and early in October Major-General Yeatman-Biggs was at Fort Lockhart, on the Samana range, with the Northampton Regiment, the 36th Sikhs, and No. 9 Mountain Battery, R.A., all of which belonged to the second division.

The date of the advance of the troops from Kohat to Shinawari had originally been fixed for early in October, but a large proportion of these troops had been employed in the operations against the Mohmands under Sir Bindon Blood—no less, in fact, than three batteries, eight infantry regiments, two companies of sappers and miners, and portions of seven field hospitals. This campaign against the Mohmands had lasted rather longer than was expected, and the advance from Kohat had consequently to be delayed; this, however, was probably far from inconvenient to the hard-worked commissariat and transport officers, who had to store a month's supplies at Kohat, besides sending on ten days' provisions to Shinawari. They were further very hard put to find the full amount of transport necessary to the requirements of each unit.

Another very great difficulty that the commissariat officers had to contend with was the want of grass for fodder in the neighbourhood of Kohat and all along the road to Shinawari.

Early in October Kohat itself was not only very hot in the middle of the day but feverish as well, and Sir William Lockhart, who had to shorten his leave in Europe to conduct the campaign before his health was completely re-established, moved up with a certain number of his staff to Fort Lockhart, on the Samana range. There the weather in October is delightful, and a good view could be obtained of the Sampagha Pass and of the preparations of the Orakzais and Afridis for resisting our advance. Meanwhile, from the 10th to the 18th of October, the movement of troops along the route from Kohat to Khusalgarh continued without intermission. But as the road became cut up with the constant traffic, the difficulties in the way of getting the over-laden " hired contractors' " and " maundagi " carts along the road, and of protecting them when broken down, continued to increase; all this only tended to confirm the belief that a light railway would confer an enormous boon in a case like this, where the ground was so favourable to its construction.

The troops already at Shinawari and Fort Lockhart, more especially the sappers and miners and the 28th Bombay Pioneers, had been working daily throughout October at improving the tracks—for one cannot call them even paths—that lead from Shinawari *via* Chagru Kotal, and from Fort Lockhart *via* Talai towards Karappa. On the 17th of October the orders for the forward movement were issued, to the effect that, on the 20th of October, Major-General Yeatman-Biggs with the 3rd Brigade (Brigadier-General Kempster's), and most of the Divisional troops should march from Shinawari *via* Chagru Kotal to Karappa. On the same day the Northampton Regiment, the 36th

Sikhs and No. 9 Mountain Battery, Royal Artillery, under Lieutenant-Colonel Chaytor, were to proceed from Fort Lockhart to Talai to protect the right flank of the other column.

On the 21st the 4th Brigade and the remaining troops of the second division were to march from Shinawari to Karappa, and Colonel Chaytor's force from Talai to Karappa, where the second division would be complete and concentrated.

On the 22nd of October the second division was to move on Khangarbur, whilst the first division, Major-General Symons's, advanced from Shinawari on Karappa. On the 23rd of October the second division was to advance to the vicinity of Ghandaki, and the first division to Karappa. Troops from the line of communication were also to move up and form the permanent garrison of Karappa as the first and second divisions advanced. A glance at the large scale map will show that these movements would have brought the first and second divisions into line ready to advance to the assault of the Sampagha Pass, the place at which, according to the information received both by the political and the intelligence officers, the Afridis and Orakzais would make a combined stand. Men and women could be seen by telescope from the Samana Range busily engaged in preparing the pass for defence by erecting sangars, or stone entrenchments, whilst the numerous watch-fires which were visible at night, both in the Khanki Valley and on the heights near the Sampagha Pass, showed that the tribesmen were concentrating their forces.

The unexpected action of the enemy, however, in advancing from the Khanki Valley and holding the portion of the Samana Range west of Chagru Kotal, the very difficult nature of the track from Chagru Kotal and Talai onwards, and the inefficiency of a large percentage of the transport animals, rendered it necessary to greatly modify the previous order for marching alluded to above.

The scale of transport allowed for this and all subsequent movements, including the march down the Bara Valley, was as follows:—

General officers, one mule and a baggage pony.

Field and staff officers, one mule.

Regimental officers, British regiments, one third mule.

Regimental officers, native regiments, half mule.

The above included the servants' kit as well, except in the case of officers of British regiments, who had a soldier instead of a native servant, and who, therefore, had not to allow for any servants' baggage in addition to their own.

For the rank and file the scale was:—

British soldiers, **one** mule to six men.

Native soldiers, one mule **to** eight men.

Followers, one mule to ten men.

In messing arrangements, British regiments were **allowed three** mules apiece; **native** regiments, **batteries,** and staff messes two, and messes of under **five one mule.**

When it is considered that a mule's load should not exceed more than about 160 lbs., that the cold in Tirah would be very great, and that native servants **as well as** their masters **would** require warm **blankets in consequence,** it will be seen, especially in **the case of** regimental officers, that there was **little allowance** except for what was absolutely necessary in the way of change **of** clothing. Beyond small *tentes d'abri,* or waterproof sheets fastened up so as to serve their purpose, tents were quite out of the question.

This restriction in the amount of baggage was necessary for the force to possess any mobility. As to tents and heavier baggage, they can follow up when the object of the movement has been attained, and the line of communications to the most advanced point has been improved and rendered more secure.

Major-General Yeatman-Biggs had his head quarters at Fort Lockhart until he moved down to Shinawari. The great fatigues and hardships he had gone through at the end of August and in the month of September, when he was engaged in constant movements up and down the Samana Range, in connection with the attacks made on Forts Gulistan, Saragarhi, and other outlying posts, had brought on a severe attack of dysentery; and though his courage was unending and his desire to be up and about intense, the disease is of so weakening a nature that he was incapable of any severe exertion on the 18th of October.

The working parties on the Chagru Kotal were at that time so continually annoyed by long-range fire from the direction of Dargai and the Narik Suk, that it became necessary to put a stop to this interruption.

Sir Power Palmer had hitherto been in command of the troops on the line of communications, including those at Shinawari, and, of all the officers with the force, was next in seniority to Sir William Lockhart. Therefore, as Major-General Yeatman-Biggs was ill, he was entrusted with the conduct of the operations, and received instructions that the Dargai and Narik Suk positions were to be cleared on October 18th.

For this purpose the second division, with the exception of the 36th Sikhs, but including the Northamptons and No. 9 Mountain Battery Royal Artillery, then at Fort Lockhart, together with the 3rd Sikhs, belonging to the first division, was placed under his orders.

The general plan of operations was to make a frontal attack from the direction of Chagru Kotal with the 4th Brigade (Brigadier-General Westmacott's), while the 3rd Brigade (Brigadier-General Kempster's), which Sir Power Palmer himself accompanied, was to attack the enemy in flank and rear, west of the Shinawari Chagru Kotal road. The latter movement necessitated a long and circuitous march over exceedingly steep and difficult hills.

In all operations in mountain warfare, when such marches are attempted, it is impossible to time the arrival of the flank attack, for unexpected difficulties, obstacles or resistance, are often met with, and the frontal attack, originally intended to be only demonstrative or a feint, has to become the real one. So it proved in this case.

Brigadier-General Kempster's brigade, with Sir Power Palmer, left the Shinawari camp at 4 A.M., and Brigadier-General Westmacott's brigade at 5 A.M.; whilst Sir William Lockhart and his staff, with an escort of the 2nd Battalion 2nd Ghoorkhas, moved out to view the operations from a point on the Samana Range, east of Chagru Kotal.

The village of Dargai lies on the northern side of a small plateau. The eastern edge of this table-land breaks off, at first, in an almost abrupt cliff; but some distance lower down, the ground, though very steep, shelves away less precipitously. This slope is thrown out from the bottom of the cliff in the form of a narrow and razor-like spur, with the path or track lying along its northern side, well within view and range of the cliff-head. But by climbing along the southern side of this spur, troops can move from Chagru Kotal, or certainly from Mama Khan, a village half-way between the former place and the plateau, unseen by the enemy.

Connecting the crest of the spur, however, and the foot of the cliff there is a narrow neck or saddle one hundred yards long by thirty broad, whose sides were far too precipitous to allow of any movement along them. Though devoid of all cover and completely exposed to the heights above, this ridge had to be crossed, so as to reach the path ascending to the summit; and here it was that the casualties in the attack by Brigadier-General Westmacott's Brigade and the heavier losses of the 20th occurred.

My description probably conveys but a very vague idea of the ground, but the illustration facing page 108, which, like all the others, has been taken from a photograph by Messrs. Law Brothers, photographers, of Kasauli and Umballa, gives a very good representation of the ground. The narrow ridge at the right-hand bottom corner is the saddle over which the rush had to be made on the 18th and 20th, and which on the latter date was simply strewn with our dead and wounded.

The enemy were posted on the top of the steep cliff seen on the left, and the illustration at page 108 shows the position from their side. Whereas the ground shelved gently away, and the huge rocks and boulders, in addition to the stone entrenchments they had erected, gave them excellent cover; on the Chagru Kotal side, as the photograph facing page 130 shows, the ground falls very steeply. The narrow track leading up this precipitous spur, however, is hardly seen in the illustration. Once the foot of the cliff is reached, the ground and most of the path up the cliff is dead or unseen from the top; unless perhaps the defenders were to very greatly expose themselves to view and to the fire, not only of the artillery, but of infantry covering the advance of their comrades from the Chagru Kotal side of the deadly ridge.

To return to the movements made by the 3rd and 4th Brigades on the 18th October, Brigadier-General Westmacott, commanding the 4th Brigade, arrived at Chagru Kotal about 9 A.M., and soon his two batteries, No. 9 Mountain Battery, Royal Artillery, and No. 5 Bombay Mountain Battery (the latter under Captain de Butts, R.A., who lost his life at the taking of the Sampagha Pass), opened fire on the ridge at a range of about eighteen hundred yards, where the enemy were to be seen clustered. The position, strengthened as it was by sangars or stone entrenchments, and only approached by the one narrow track, was practically impregnable if resolutely held. But it was hoped that Brigadier-General Kempster's column, making the flank attack, would soon appear on the enemy's right flank and rear, and render a frontal attack unnecessary, except as a demonstration. The appearance of this flanking column was therefore eagerly looked for from the commanding position on the Samana Range, where Sir William Lockhart and his staff were posted.

The frontal attack was made by the infantry, with the 1st Battalion 3rd Ghoorkhas leading, the King's Own Scottish Borderers (K.O.S.B.'s) supporting them, and the Northampton Regiment (the old 48th of Peninsular fame) in reserve.

First Action of Dargai.

The infantry had to make their way in extended order along the precipitous hillside on the western and southern slopes of the spur, till the point was reached where no further advance was possible except under the close view and fire of the enemy. Every point of vantage, meanwhile, had been occupied in order to bring fire to bear on such of the enemy as showed themselves on the ridge, and finally about 12 noon the little Ghoorkhas, led by their officers, and closely backed up by the K.O.S.B.'s, could be seen streaming across the ridge.

The enemy had been keeping up an intermittent fire, from about 9.30 A.M., till now; but, as soon as the Ghoorkhas appeared boldly advancing across the open space, every rifle, smooth-bore, and "jezail" (or native firearm) on the cliff above, blazed away. So sudden was the rush, and so well prepared had it been both by artillery and infantry fire, that in crossing the ridge only sixteen of the Ghoorkhas and six K.O.S.B.'s were hit, two of the former and one of the latter being killed. The Northamptons had been kept in reserve further back; and the 36th Sikhs, the 4th Regiment of Brigadier-General Westmacott's

Brigade, who were burning to avenge the death and mutilation of their twenty-one comrades who had fallen at Saragarhi, had been obliged, much to their chagrin, to remain at Fort Lockhart, to help the 2nd Battalion 2nd Ghoorkhas there, in garrisoning the forts.

Although by 12 o'clock noon the flank attack by Brigadier-General Kempster's Brigade had not been delivered, still the moral effect of it had doubtless been felt, and to this cause too must be attributed the wonderfully small losses we suffered.

The spectacle of the 3rd Ghoorkhas rushing across the dangerous zone on the ridge, and of the K.O.S.B.'s, who had started 800 yards behind them when the attack began, straining every nerve to catch up and even pass them was a stirring sight; and the advance up the cliff side, led by Lieutenant Beynon, D.S.O. (the author of that excellent book "With Kelly to Chitral"), with a revolver in one hand and a climbing-stick or alpenstock in the other, was a thing to be ever remembered.

The attack on Dargai on the 18th October was rather lost sight of and forgotten in the more tragic events of the second attack on the 20th October, but it must be remembered that when the 1st Battalion 3rd Ghoorkhas advanced over the ridge to the attack, the enemy, for all our troops knew, might be in overwhelming strength, and prepared to stand till the last; and the bravery of the 1st Battalion 3rd Ghoorkhas, and that of the K.O.S.B.'s, who followed them with such eagerness, should not, because the losses were fortunately small, be too much overshadowed by the magnificent courage shown by the 2nd Battalion 2nd Ghoorkhas and the Gordon Highlanders and other regiments two days later. The enemy did not stop on the top of the cliff to await Lieutenant Beynon's arrival, and that of the men crowding behind him, but fled precipitately, and the tower of Dargai village, a few hundred yards on, was soon seen to be in flames.

It is now time to turn to Brigadier-General Kempster's movements. Great as were the difficulties reported of the precipitous mountain sides over which this column had to advance, they exceeded all expectations. It was found quite impossible even to take any mules with them, and the force therefore, without any mountain battery, and only retaining stretchers and dhoolies (the latter being covered-in litters carried by native dhooly bearers), struggled up the mountain side, led by the 2nd Battalion 2nd Ghoorkhas, who are never more at home than when they are working over rugged broken ground.

Any one who has seen a mountain battery in India going over the roughest and steepest ground, and the astonishing manner in which laden mules will go along a path which one would imagine to be only fitted for goats, will appreciate how very difficult and steep a mountain side must be when no mules can accompany the infantry; it was so in this case however. It was soon after twelve noon that the 4th Brigade seized the Dargai ridge; and as the enemy, not waiting the actual assault, began to stream away from it, they came under the fire of the leading troops of Brigadier-General Kempster's column, and suffered some loss. The two brigades then joined hands at Dargai. About 2.30 P.M. the regiments of the 4th Brigade began to move down the spur again, followed at about 4.30 P.M. by the troops under Brigadier-General Kempster's command. Attracted by the sound of the firing, the Afridis, estimated as 8,000 strong, could be seen hastening up from the Khanki Valley, and Brigadier-General Kempster had to undertake that most difficult operation of war, a retirement in the face of overwhelming numbers; for the tribesmen turned out of the position by Brigadier-General Westmacott had begun to return and to join hands with the newly arrived Afridis. It was not deemed advisable by Sir William Lockhart to hold the position; and in connection with this point I cannot do better than quote from a letter written five days afterwards to the *Times* by their special correspondent with the force:—

"The question at once suggests itself, why surrender the position having once captured it? It may perhaps be admitted at once that, knowing then all that we know now, *e.g.*, the resolution of the enemy and the fact that water is to be found in the locality, it would have been better to retain the position won. But, on the other hand, there is always great risk in isolating detachments to occupy remote posts like these, and there is immense difficulty in arranging adequately and in time for their food and water.

"They are liable moreover to be surrounded and attacked on all sides by the enemy, and then must in their turn be relieved or supported, and thus attention and strength are diverted to side issues, and complications are apt to arise which become a source of weakness and of anxieties. Such are some of the considerations which no doubt induced Sir William Lockhart not to place a detachment on the Narik Suk, and the very fact that it was re-occupied in greater strength than ever by the enemy as soon as we withdrew from it, shows that any troops left there on the night of the 18th would at once have been fiercely attacked."

The Gordon Highlanders and the 15th Sikhs were the two last regiments to retire from Dargai, and on these fell the brunt of the fighting which now ensued.

The enemy pressed boldly down the hill following up the troops, but point after point was held by separate companies to cover the retirement of the others. It was getting dusk too, and though for a time the batteries on Chagru Kotal were of the greatest service in keeping back any bodies of the tribesmen who offered too conspicuous a mark, their fire had ultimately to cease.

The enemy lost heavily; so heavily that, as soon as the troops had reached Chagru Kotal at the foot of the spur, the movement thence on to Shinawari was absolutely unmolested.

Major Jennings-Bramley, of the Gordon Highlanders, was most unfortunately killed in this affair, and Lieutenant Pears, of the Cameronians attached to that regiment, severely wounded. The losses were, in addition to these:—

Gordon Highlanders	2 killed,	15 wounded.
1st Battalion 2nd Ghoorkhas	1 ,,	4 ,,
3rd Sikhs	— ,,	1 ,,
15th Sikhs	3 ,,	11 ,,
Followers	— ,,	3 ,,

The total losses in this day's fight, including those of the 4th Brigade, were ten killed and fifty-three wounded.

The rearguard of these troops, who had been under arms since 4 A.M., and who, in the case of Brigadier-General Kempster's column, had done the most difficult climbing, only reached camp at Shinawari at 11 P.M. that night, having been nineteen hours under arms. The wisdom of sending back all the mules to camp became very apparent when the very difficult movement from Dargai to Chagru Kotal had to be begun, and Sir Power Palmer, in his dispatch to Sir William Lockhart, showed his appreciation of the excellent behaviour and handling of the troops when he said, "The force, unhampered by transport, and assisted by the faultless dispositions made by Kempster and the steadiness of the troops, British and native, were able to inflict considerable loss on the enemy, so much so, that our return to camp at Shinawari was quite unmolested." The fact that when once the troops had reached Chagru Kotal the enemy ceased all further attack is a very clear proof that he must have suffered heavily, for otherwise the return to camp from Chagru Kotal might have resulted in some more severe fighting.

CHAPTER VII.

THE ATTACK ON DARGAI OF THE 20TH OCTOBER.

THE advance of the second division from Shinawari on Karappa began to take place on the 20th October, as previously ordered.

It had been intended by Sir William Lockhart that the second division should send a working party up to the Chagru Kotal on the 19th to continue the work on the road, from that place to Karappa; but Major-General Yeatman-Biggs, who had now moved down from Fort Lockhart to Shinawari, considered that the troops of the second division were too much exhausted by what they had gone through on the 18th in the assault on Dargai to justify him in employing them in covering working parties, and the heliogram conveying this information to the chief of the staff reached Sir William Lockhart too late to enable troops to be sent from Fort Lockhart for this purpose.

Late on the evening of the 19th a telegram from

Shinawari told Sir William Lockhart that a large gathering of tribesmen was visible on the Dargai position, and that Major-General Yeatman-Biggs proposed moving on Karappa, *via* Gulistan Fort, instead of down the Chagru defile. Sir William Lockhart, however, ordered the original route to be adhered to, remarking that, while it would probably be necessary to clear the enemy off the Dargai heights, they would very likely retire, to prevent their line of retreat being threatened, as soon as troops pushing down the Chagru road reached the point where a ravine running from below the Narik Suk, the hill above Dargai, joins the Chagru defile.

In order to strengthen the force which Major-General Yeatman-Biggs would have at his disposal for offensive purposes, if the enemy held on to the Dargai position, Sir William Lockhart placed under his orders two battalions and a battery of the first division. These were the 2nd Battalion Derbyshire Regiment (the old 95th), the 3rd Sikhs and No. 1 (Kohat) Mountain Battery.

The advance guard under Brigadier-General Kempster left camp Shinawari at 4.30 A.M., and

THE DARGAI POSITION FROM ENEMY'S SIDE.

[To face page 130.

Second Action of Dargai.

about 9 A.M. the whole of the troops under Major-General Yeatman-Biggs were massed on, or near, the Chagru Kotal. The Northampton Regiment and No. 9 Mountain Battery Royal Artillery were also by this time on the Samana Suk, east of the Chagru Kotal, and about level with, and 2,500 yards distant from, the Dargai crest. The enemy were seen to be holding this position in great force, but a still more numerous body of them could be seen on a ridge farther to the south, overlooking the track by which Brigadier-General Kempster had brought his column up on the 18th.

The tribesmen evidently expected a flank attack from this direction, not only because of the one previously delivered from that side, but because Mr. Donald, the political officer with the second division, who thoroughly understands the Pathan, and more particularly the Orakzai, had confided to his native spies, as an absolutely dead secret, and in the full confidence that they would at once divulge it, the information that another flank attack would be carried out. The spies, of course, at once informed their fellow-tribesmen, who, acting on what they considered such very excellent information, took every precaution to meet this mythical attack on their right flank.

Having arrived at Chagru Kotal, Major-General Yeatman-Biggs decided to take the position by a frontal attack, and orders were given to Brigadier-General Kempster to carry this out. The latter officer sent forward for this purpose the 1st Battalion 2nd Ghoorkhas in first line, the 1st Battalion Dorset Regiment (the old 39th) in second line, and the Derbyshire Regiment (95th) in the third line. The Gordon Highlanders (75th) were to assist the advance, if necessary, by long range volleys from a village called Mama Khan, about half-way between Chagru Kotal and Dargai, whilst the 3rd Sikhs remained as escort to the guns at Chagru Kotal. The mountain batteries present were No. 8 Mountain Battery, Royal Artillery, No. 5 Bombay Mountain Battery, and No. 1 Kohat Mountain Battery, while No. 9 Mountain Battery, Royal Artillery, was on the hill above, so that there were twenty-four guns in all. With the 1st Battalion 2nd Ghoorkhas were Lieutenant Tillard, and the scouts of the 1st Battalion 3rd Ghoorkhas. These scouts are

Second Action of Dargai.

men from some Ghoorkha regiments, mountaineers by birth, who have been specially trained to move very quickly over the hill-sides. The extra training given them is much the same as that which a professional trainer might give a man whom he thought likely to develop into a good runner. They were more lightly equipped than the other Ghoorkhas, and carried fewer rounds of ammunition, so that with their light equipment, fleetness of foot, and good wind and condition, they were, all through the campaign, formidable rivals even to the Pathan in his native hills.

It could clearly be seen with glasses that the enemy had strongly "sangared" or fortified the whole edge of the cliff, and that they were exceedingly numerous, both on the side of the real attack and also on their right flank, where they expected another attack, which never came. The guns opened fire about 10 A.M., at a range of about 1,800 yards, the battery on the Samana Suk above them joining in at a range of about 2,500 yards. Soon afterwards, as the Ghoorkhas pressed along the spur leading up to Dargai, keeping as much under cover as possible, the enemy began to open fire, though they were given but little mark to shoot at, and when the Ghoorkhas had advanced to within effective rifle range, about five hundred yards or so from the crest where the enemy were posted, they in turn opened fire.

The Dorset Regiment were meanwhile closing on the Ghoorkhas, and a temporary halt was made behind the watershed, which concealed our troops from the enemy's fire. Lieutenant-Colonel Travers was commanding the 1st Battalion 2nd Ghoorkhas, a regiment famous for its exploits on the ridge before Delhi in the Mutiny days, and for its valour during the last Afghan war, in consequence of which it was allowed the distinction of wearing the Prince of Wales' plume. Knowing how important it was that the zone of fire through which they would have to go should be crossed as rapidly as possible, Lieutenant-Colonel Travers had decided to lead the left half battalion or left wing across himself, leaving the right half battalion to follow under Major Judge, the second in command.

Turning to Lieutenant Tillard, with the 3rd Ghoorkha scouts, to Captain Macintyre and Captain Bower (attached), and to his adjutant, Captain Norie, to ask them if they were all ready, he gave the signal to advance, and the officers all dashed forward. Followed by their men, and with the loss of about thirty, they reached some dead ground, where they were temporarily safe.

Major Judge, with the remaining wing, rose to follow, but the moment he appeared above the crest he was shot dead. Captain Robinson was also mortally wounded, and died a few days afterwards.

The bullets were raining like hail on the space which had to be crossed, for the enemy, a little taken by surprise by the rush of the leading wing, were now fully on the alert. So, many a brave little Ghoorkha bit the dust. Both Derbys and Dorsets vainly attempted to follow, but the enemy were as yet quite unshaken by the artillery fire, and to advance into the hail of bullets was almost certain death. Not deterred by this, many brave officers and men, singly or in little groups, attempted the task; but few succeeded in reaching the Ghoorkhas untouched.

Captain Arnold (Dorsetshire Regiment) was dangerously wounded as he rose from cover to lead his company forward, and Lieutenant Hewett, of the same regiment, led a section or quarter company forward, and he alone got across, with his sword-scabbard shot away and a bullet-graze on the elbow; every man in the section following him was killed. Single men of both regiments occasionally got across, and many a Dorsetshire and Derbyshire man sallied forth into the deadly zone to try and drag in a wounded comrade, and in most cases paid for his courage with his life. The only chance for a wounded man was to lie perfectly still; if he moved or attempted to crawl into safety, bullets showered on and round him. Private Vickery, of the Dorset Regiment, to whom I shall again allude, made repeated, and finally successful efforts to bring in a wounded comrade, and he appeared to bear a charmed life.

To take the position was an impossibility till the artillery had played continuously on it, and reinforcements arrived. The guns, it is true, had been firing throughout, but only intermittently; for, so well concealed was the enemy, and so difficult was the position to "range in," that is, to see exactly whether the shells were bursting short or over, that it was impossible to know if they were doing any damage.

It was now long past noon. Only six miles out of a thirteen-mile march had been covered, and the animals, loaded up before daylight, were still standing under their burdens. Major-General Yeatman-Biggs sent to Brigadier-General Kempster and told him that the position must be taken at all costs. The latter officer took the Gordon Highlanders and the 3rd Sikhs forward. A wait of nearly an hour, and then there were four regiments with bayonets fixed, ready, as soon as the moment arrived, to push on up to where the 2nd Ghoorkhas were waiting, and with them to force a way up the narrow path.

Brigadier-General Kempster took the wise precaution of ordering every available gun to keep up for three minutes as hot and rapid a fire as possible, at the end of which time the Gordon Highlanders, followed by the 3rd Sikhs, were to advance over the ridge, now thickly strewn with dead and dying. For three minutes every gun rained shells on to the position, and then Colonel Mathias led his Highlanders forward. With the pipes playing "Cock o' the North," and with

Colonel Mathias, Major Forbes Macbean, and Lieutenant A. F. Gordon at the head of the leading company, the old 75th dashed into the open space, backed up by the 3rd Sikhs. The remaining Derbys and Dorsets joined in, forming an indiscriminate mass, and all pressed forward to where the Ghoorkhas had been awaiting this reinforcement since they had made their first rush some hours before. A pause for breath, and then the second advance was made up into the position, Lieutenant Cowie, of the Dorset Regiment, being the first to reach the summit.

Great as were the losses, the concentrated artillery fire, and the suddenness of the rush had undoubtedly tended to make the enemy's fire a little less terrible than it had been after the Ghoorkhas had first advanced, but, even so, the casualties were very heavy.

Lance-Corporal Milne, leading the Highland Pipers, was hit the moment he appeared at the head of them; and Piper Findlater, though shot through both legs, continued, while sitting wounded on the ground, to play his pipes undauntedly. The enemy again did not await the actual onslaught, and when the leading troops had reached the top of the cliff they could be seen streaming away in the direction of the Khanki Valley.

Among the incidents connected with the charge of the Gordons, I must mention that Major F. Macbean was wounded dangerously as soon as the first rush began, and while lying on the ground continued to cheer on his men.

Some conspicuous acts of valour and devotion were performed. Private Lawson, Gordon Highlanders, rushed into the hail of bullets and carried Lieutenant Dingwall, who was wounded and unable to move, into a place of safety; he then returned into the fire zone and carried back a disabled comrade, being wounded himself in two places while so doing.

When Captain W. E. C. Smith, of the Derbyshire Regiment fell, Lieutenant H. S. Pennell, of the same regiment, endeavoured, under a murderous fire, to carry him into a place of safety, and only when he found that Captain Smith was dead did he desist from his efforts.

Nor was it by any means only British officers and men who performed conspicuous acts of gallantry, for a native officer of the 1st Battalion 2nd Ghoorkhas, Kirpa Ram Thapa by name, though wounded in two places, refused to fall out, and continued to command his company.

Many other gallant deeds were done, too numerous to chronicle; and many a Victoria Cross was fairly earned, but not won, either because the man who performed it did not happen to be observed by any one in authority, or because he died in the execution of it.

There were many marvellous escapes this day, both amongst officers and men. Captain Bower, attached to the 1st Battalion 2nd Ghoorkhas, had his sword scabbard shot away; and so had Lieutenant Hewett, of the Dorset Regiment. Major Downman, Gordon Highlanders, had a bullet through his helmet; and Lieutenant Dingwall, of the same regiment, was hit four times—one bullet struck his revolver and another his cartridge case, exploding the cartridges, and two bullets then hit him on the knee, but, despite this, in a few weeks he was up and about.

The following were the losses in the various regiments engaged that day:—

Second Action of Dargai.   141

Derbyshire Regiment.—Killed: Captain W. E. C. Smith and three men; wounded, eight men.

Dorsetshire Regiment.— Killed: Nine men; wounded, Captain W. R. Arnold, Lieutenant J. C. Hewett, and thirty-nine men.

Gordon Highlanders.—Killed: Lieutenant A. Lamont and two men; wounded, Lieutenant-Colonel H. H. Mathias, C.B., Major F. Macbean, Captain H. P. Uniacke, Lieutenants K. Dingwall, M. F. M. Meiklejohn, G. S. G. Craufurd, and thirty-five men.

1st Battalion 2nd Ghoorkhas.—Killed: Major Judge, Captain Robinson, and sixteen men; wounded, forty-nine men.

3rd Sikhs.— Killed: Three men; wounded, Lieutenant White and sixteen men.

Total casualties, 193.

Of the officers, a good many were only grazed or very slightly wounded, and Lieutenant-Colonel Mathias, Captain Uniacke, Lieutenants Meiklejohn, Hewett, and Craufurd were all fit for duty a very few days afterwards.

The three minutes' continuous artillery fire, followed by the magnificent rush of the Gordon

Highlanders, backed up by the 3rd Sikhs, just gave the other tired troops the impetus which was necessary; and the very heavy casualties sustained by the 1st Battalion 2nd Ghoorkhas and the Dorsetshire Regiment show what a hot fire both these regiments had sustained before the Gordons and the 3rd Sikhs advanced.

The 1st Battalion 2nd Ghoorkhas and the Dorsetshire Regiment were left on the position, or rather on the Narik Suk, the hill above it, to hold it for the night, whilst the other troops descended the hill again to the Chagru Kotal.

As the Ghoorkhas, dead and wounded, were lying thickly scattered here and there, while the bulk of the regiment had to remain on the hill above, the Gordon Highlanders and men of other British regiments helped to carry their stricken and helpless comrades down the hill, a friendly act which tended to cement more than ever the great sympathy which has always existed between Ghoorkhas and their British fellow-soldiers. Sepoys of other native regiments frequently strike up great friendships with men of British regiments with whom they are thrown in contact; but their language, habits, and customs are so different that the intercourse between them, though most friendly, is necessarily restricted. With a Ghoorkha it is very different; he is dressed like our riflemen at home, he loves sport and games, he smokes a pipe, and drinks a pint of beer with the greatest gusto; in fact he is never so happy as when he is thrown together with a British regiment.

It was getting dusk by the time the troops had got back to the Chagru Kotal, and impossible to continue the march that day; the men had therefore to bivouac on and around that place. As the transport animals coming up from Shinawari had been absolutely blocked by the halt made at Chagru Kotal, many of the regiments were unable to get their great-coats and blankets. They had no food beyond that which they had taken in their haversacks, and water and wood were very difficult to get, and in some places absolutely unprocurable; the troops, therefore, especially those on the hills above Chagru Kotal, spent a most trying and comfortless night in the bitter cold, the elevation of the Samana Suk and of the Narik Suk, just above Chagru Kotal, being nearly seven thousand feet.

It is impossible to estimate the enemy's losses. Many blood-stains were found on the ground, but in a fight of this sort, where the enemy has no intention of letting his assailant come hand to hand, a proportion of unarmed men, women, and boys are always ready to carry off a dead or wounded man.

A Pathan has the greatest horror of his dead falling into an enemy's hands, for fear the body should be burnt or even singed, either of which contingencies would, a Pathan Mahommedan imagines, prevent his admission into Paradise; and this is the reason why he is always anxious, if possible, to burn the body of a foeman.

Sir William Lockhart had intimated to the general officer commanding the second division his belief that "if troops were pushed on to the junction of the Narik defile and the Chagru defile on the road towards Karappa, the enemy would probably retire on finding his rear threatened."

The original orders for the 20th had been that the 3rd Brigade and only some of the divisional troops, second division, should move on that day to Karappa, the 4th Brigade and the remaining divisional troops following on the 21st; but these orders had been modified, and the whole second division had been ordered to move from Shinawari to Karappa on the 20th.

Major-General Yeatman-Biggs therefore had at his disposal on the 20th, the 2nd Battalion K.O.S.B.'s, the 1st Battalion 3rd Ghoorkhas of the 4th Brigade, and the Jhind Imperial Service Infantry. Counting the two regiments and the battery of the division lent him, he had nine regiments of infantry and four batteries of artillery (without reckoning the Northampton Regiment, who were available for protecting his right flank from the Samana Suk). He might therefore, had he wished and thought fit to do so, have pushed troops along the road to Karappa and threatened the enemy's rear, in which case possibly the frontal attack need only have been a demonstrative one.

Sir William Lockhart, as his despatches show, certainly intended that a flank attack should be made, but he adds in his despatch: "At the same time I recognise that the enemy's defeat was rendered more complete and decisive by their being encouraged to hold on till the last, and the result of the action must be regarded as satisfactory, inasmuch as the movement of the troops' baggage and supplies from Shinawari to Karappa, subsequent to the capture of the Dargai heights, was almost unmolested."

It may be that I have done little justice to the valour of the troops engaged, but the photographs of the ground over which they had to fight and the actual losses they suffered tell their tale in far better language than I can command.

CHAPTER VIII.

THE MOVE INTO THE KHANKI VALLEY AND THE ASSAULT ON THE SAMPAGHA AND ARHANGA PASSES.

THE forward movement from Chagru Kotal to Karappa was resumed on the 21st of October; whilst the troops also began to move from Fort Lockhart, on the Samana Range, to Karappa on that date. In the latter case the forces consisted of the Northampton Regiment, the 36th Sikhs, No. 9 M.B.R.A. and No. 3 Company, Bombay Sappers and Miners. They were joined *en route* by the 21st Madras Pioneers, who had spent a terribly cold night on the Samana Suk hill without food, beyond what little was left over in their haversacks, and without blankets, great-coats, or fuel. This must have been a trying experience to a Madras regiment, the men of which are quite unaccustomed to the cold of Northern India, more especially at an altitude of some 7,000 feet.

The troops marching from Fort Lockhart, whom

Sir William Lockhart and his staff accompanied, found the road fairly good as far as Talai, about half-way to Karappa; and this was largely owing to the fact that working parties had greatly improved it for some way down. But after Talai, the path became most difficult till the Khanki Valley was reached; it was little more than a goat track going down a very steep mountain side through thick scrub and bushes. A company of sappers and miners had to be busily at work cutting it away and removing boulders in order to allow the transport animals which were following to get along without their loads being brushed off.

The column was a very small one (three regiments, a company of sappers, and a battery); all the baggage was on a reduced scale, and what little resistance there was on reaching the neighbourhood of Karappa was quickly overcome by the troops of the main column, and did not in the least affect the progress of the Fort Lockhart column; nevertheless the 36th Sikhs, under Lieut.-Colonel Haughton, who were on rearguard duty, only managed to reach Talai, half-way, and that at 2.39 A.M. next morning. They did not reach

Camp Karappa till 6.30 P.M. the next evening, having been actually thirty hours or more engaged in marching a distance of twelve miles, and down hill the whole time.

But this delay on the road was also very largely due to the inefficient transport. The Northampton Regiment were supplied with indifferent mules and ponies, and the 36th Sikhs only had donkeys; so, what with loads slipping, and animals falling and blocking the way, the pace of the rearguard in the worst parts of the road seldom exceeded a few hundred yards an hour.

The second division, main column, moving by the lower road, experienced just as much difficulty; and in their case it was several days before all the baggage and supplies reached the camp.

The difficulty of moving in such mountainous country, where there are no roads, is enormous; more particularly when one transport driver has to attend to three beasts. As these animals reach places where they must jump, slip, or scramble down from one rock to another, some accident is bound to happen before long to the loads, no matter how well they have been put on. Frequently it happens that there is no room to draw aside from the so-called track to readjust loads; then everything is stopped; and when there are about twenty thousand transport animals, the number of these breakdowns is everlasting.

The troops, who had spent the night on Dargai and on the adjoining hill, moved down the spur in a line parallel with the march of the main second division behind them; and as they descended they burnt the village towers, the inhabitants of which had been annoying the working parties on the Chagru Kotal some days before.

Karappa itself was not found suitable as a camping ground, as it was commanded within easy range by high hills; the camp was, therefore, fixed near Khangarbur, some two miles further on, where there was a most excellent site. As the leading troops of the main column approached Khangarbur, some tribesmen opened fire, but they were easily dispersed by a few rounds from a mountain battery.

Although the camp was not very near Karappa, it was nevertheless termed Camp Karappa, Khangarbur being on the other side of the river.

All through the evening of the 21st, troops and baggage kept filing into camp, and soon nearly all had arrived, but as the whole ground was covered with bushes which there had not been time to cut down or to make roads through, it was a very difficult matter indeed to find out where to go. Many an officer and man therefore had to do without his baggage or blankets that night, either because the animals had not arrived, or because, as was frequently the case, the baggage parties had no time to find out the portion of the camp allotted to them. Still, every precaution was taken to make the camp secure against a night attack and to assist belated men and transport animals in getting in.

Regiments kept sounding the bugle calls at intervals; a strong guard was posted below the entrance to the camp, to protect as far as possible the transport which still kept coming in; as regards the very large proportion of it which was blocked further back on both roads, arrangements had been made to stop any further forward movement and to camp *en route*, surrounded by a strong guard.

It was very much warmer at Karappa than it

had been on the Samana Range, and from the 21st till the 28th the time was spent in concentrating the two divisions, for, owing to the two actions of Dargai, the extreme difficulty of the road, and the inefficiency of some of the transport, the programme of moves issued on the 17th October was greatly upset.

The time between the 21st and the 28th was also spent in strengthening and clearing the camp, in completing the supplies required for the forward movement, and in improving, as far as possible, the dirty and muddy supply of drinking water. The surrounding country was also foraged for grain and fodder, towers and defences were destroyed, and the country in the direction of the Sampagha Pass was carefully reconnoitred.

On the evening of the 27th, both divisions, with the exception of the 30th Punjaub Infantry, who had been left to hold Dargai, were concentrated at Camp Karappa ready for a forward movement. The enemy, however, had been very far from idle during all this time. Hardly had we settled down in camp on the evening of the 21st October than they began firing into it at long ranges from the surrounding hills; and from Khangarbur, especially, no foraging party went out but that it was followed up when it retired, and fired on from the heights above. Casualties always occurred both when foraging and from the sniping, which was continued on the nights of the 21st, 22nd and 23rd.

Information had been received that a night attack would be made on the 24th. But, considering a large portion of the first division had now joined the second division, it seemed improbable that the enemy would have deferred a night attack till our numbers were so augmented, and the defences round the camp had been so vastly improved.

The night, however, passed without any firing; much less was any attempt made to rush the camp.

The 25th was perhaps the worst night of the whole time until the troops regained British territory near Peshawur. The first division had sent a strong foraging party out that day, which was continually fired upon as it returned, resulting in some thirteen casualties. Emboldened perhaps by their success, the enemy, contrary to their usual practice, began to fire into camp before it was dusk, and from 4 P.M. to 10 P.M. or so bullets were flying thick and fast, this was continued at intervals all through the night, and resulted in some twenty-two casualties.

Captain Badcock, D.S.O., an Intelligence Officer on the Headquarter Staff, was hit through the arm whilst sitting at lunch with several other officers, the limb having to be amputated; and Lieutenant Crocker, orderly officer to Brigadier-General Kempster, received a severe contusion on the shoulder from a spent bullet. Also, while at lunch, there were many very narrow escapes, as was only natural: and hardly had some sacks of grain been hastily piled round Sir William Lockhart's tent than they were hit by two bullets. In the morning two British soldiers and four native followers were found outside the camp, so cut up as to be quite unrecognisable.

On the 25th, all, or nearly all, the success was with the enemy, for the tribesmen, both in firing on the foraging parties and into camp, were careful not to group together so as to offer any mark either for artillery fire or musketry volleys. Occasionally at nights when the constant firing led it to be imagined that they might be in considerable numbers and close by, a battery would be ordered to fire a star shell to light up the surrounding darkness, and enable the infantry to pour in a volley; but it seldom happened that the assailants could be seen. Even if two or three of them were for a moment visible, a volley fired when it was impossible to see along the sights of a rifle was not very apt to go near the mark, much less to hit it.

After the night of the 25th the system was adopted of picketing the surrounding hills with forces of not less than a company or a very strong half company—in all cases well entrenched; and this was continued till the end of the first phase of the campaign. By this method, pickets are secure against attack when entrenched behind sangars on the tops of hills; and when the guards are sufficiently strong and the ground around the positions has been prepared with wire entanglements they are safe from being rushed. With a ring of these pickets the firing into camp was attended with a considerable amount of danger to the tribesmen, more especially as the enterprising Ghoorkha scouts, commanded by Captain Lucas and Lieutenants Bruce and Tillard, were continually out in small parties stalking the disturbers of our repose. After we arrived at Maidan the night-firing diminished in a notable manner. This was partly due, without doubt, to the intense cold, but the result was largely attributed to the Ghoorkha scouts, who proved highly successful in shooting or cutting up unwary Afridi sportsmen.

The casualties from the night-firing into camp also diminished for another reason. After the heavy losses of the night of the 25th, both officers and men either dug a sleeping-place in the ground or piled up stones around it, whilst those regiments or groups of staff officers who had not a house for their mess, made a rough bullet-proof wall round the places where they dined; consequently, when they were either at dinner or asleep it was almost impossible for them to be hit by a bullet.

Nothing of this sort, however, could be done for the transport animals; and there was seldom a night, at the beginning of the campaign, but that one or more of them was hit. The native followers were constantly warned of the danger of sitting round a camp fire after dark, and of the advisability of constructing some stone shelter round their sleeping-places; but they invariably preferred, with the indolence and belief in fate so common amongst Orientals, to stand the chance of being shot rather than exert themselves to pile up stones or forego the genial warmth of a fire.

The night of the 26th and 27th passed without much further firing into camp, so excellent was the system of pickets now adopted; the resistance to the foraging parties was also less severe.

There were altogether a good many casualties during our stay at Karappa. Lieutenant-Colonel Hadow, 15th Sikhs, was shot through the leg while out reconnoitring, and the total casualties were three officers wounded, and twenty-five British and twenty-one native soldiers killed and wounded. A large number of followers and of animals must also have been hit.

On the 28th of October both divisions moved forward to Camp Ghandaki; the 30th Punjaub Infantry of the 1st Brigade still remaining at

Dargai, and the 21st Madras Pioneers at Karappa, so as to help the troops on the line of communication to garrison it.

The 1st Division advanced along the plain to Ghandaki, some miles distant; and so did the 3rd Brigade; while the 4th Brigade and the remainder of the 2nd Division moved along the river bed or west of it. East of Ghandaki and north of Karappa was a very steep hill, which had been constantly held by the enemy, and from which the tribesmen used to descend at night to fire into Camp Karappa. This hill was most successfully seized by the Northampton Regiment and the 36th Sikhs under Colonel Chaytor, commanding the former regiment. The force, starting from camp at 5 A.M., were on the hill before the enemy, who had apparently slept in Ghandaki village, had time to get up there and resist the advance.

As soon as the 1st Division arrived at Ghandaki, a reconnaissance was made towards the Sampagha Pass, in which Lieutenant-Colonel Sage of the 2nd Battalion 1st Ghoorkhas was wounded, the other casualties of the day being two men killed and ten wounded.

On the night of the 28th orders were issued to advance and attack the Sampagha Pass the next day. Viewed from the plain below, the range over which the pass leads has two large spurs projecting to the south, one on each side of the plateau on which Ghandaki is situated; so that one seemed to be at the bottom of a huge amphitheatre, of which the lower sides sloped gently down and were intersected by nullahs in all directions, while further up, they rose very precipitously.

There appeared to be four paths crossing the range fairly close together, of which the one termed the Sampagha seemed much the easiest, and it was against this that the main attack was to be directed.

The enemy's watch fires were seen in large numbers on the night of the 28th, not only round the pass itself, but on the spur west of our camp, on their right flank, against which they evidently expected us to conduct a turning movement. No such measure, however, was contemplated. Our plan of attack, shortly stated, was to send one regiment of the 1st Brigade to guard the left flank of the main line of advance, while another regiment of the same brigade similarly guarded the right flank. The third and remaining regiment (the 4th Regiment of the brigade being at Dargai) was to seize and hold for the artillery a hill opposite the centre of the position, and under cover of the artillery fire to drive the remaining three brigades like a wedge into the centre of the position. These tactics succeeded admirably, though the enemy's resistance was but feeble; and by 11 A.M. the pass was in our hands.

At 5 A.M. the regiments of the 1st Brigade (Brigadier-General Hart's) left camp, the 1st Battalion Devonshire Regiment (the old 11th) making for and seizing a village on the right flank of the advance. The 2nd Battalion 1st Ghoorkhas in like manner occupied a village on the left flank, and the 2nd Battalion Derbyshire Regiment (95th) seized the hill designed as the first artillery position.

These movements, so important for the ultimate success of the operations, were executed without the very slightest hitch, and the flanks of the advancing column were absolutely protected during the whole advance. Following the 1st Brigade, moved the artillery of both divisions, six batteries in all, and a rocket detachment under Captain Browne, R.A. The 2nd Brigade, Brigadier-General Gaselee's, the 4th Brigade, General Westmacott's, and the 3rd Brigade, Brigadier-General Kempster's, then followed each other in the order named.

The baggage was all left in camp under a guard of one squadron of the 18th Bengal Lancers, and a battalion of Nabha Imperial Service Infantry, with orders to move on after the troops as soon as heliographic orders to do so arrived. All the artillery was under the command of Brigadier-General Spragg, R.A., and he brought the three batteries of the 1st Division under Lieut.-Colonel Duthy, R.A., into action on the hill previously seized by the Derbyshire Regiment, who now remained as escort to the guns. These three batteries made beautiful practice against a large "sangar" covering the beginning of the zigzag road up the pass, and under cover of this fire the 2nd Brigade (Brigadier-General Gaselee's) advanced, accompanied by Major-General Symons, with the 3rd Sikhs on the right, the Yorkshire Regiment (19th) right centre, the Queen's Royal West Surrey (2nd) left centre, and the 2nd Battalion 4th Ghoorkhas on the left, while the 4th Brigade followed closely with the 3rd Brigade behind them.

The batteries opened fire about 7.30 A.M., and as the enemy began to evacuate the "sangar," which the shells were hitting time after time, and as the 2nd Brigade were nearing the crest of what I may term the enemy's advanced post, and on which the guns had been playing, Brigadier-General Spragg sent forward the three batteries of the 2nd Division under Lieut.-Colonel Purdy to a more advanced position, to cover the movement of the 2nd Brigade against the main ridge, on which there were several sangars.

The ground over which the 2nd Brigade had to advance was very stony and precipitous, but the whole line pressed steadily on, and by 9.45 A.M. the Queen's (who were the first up), and the other three regiments of the brigade, had captured the dip in the ridge on which the Sampagha Pass is situated. The guns of the 2nd Division had burst shell after shell on the top of this ridge before the

Assault on the Sampagha Pass. 163

infantry gained it: and, although, possibly owing to the great steepness of the reverse slopes, comparatively little physical damage was done to the enemy, the moral effect was undoubtedly great, and prevented them lining the crest to oppose the infantry advance.

When the pass had been taken the enemy still clung to the heights above it on each side, and the 3rd Sikhs and the Yorkshire Regiment were sent off to crown the hill on the right, while the 2nd Battalion 4th Ghoorkhas were sent against the hill on the left, and two companies of the Queen's, with the scouts of the 3rd and 5th Ghoorkhas, worked up a spur between the Yorkshire Regiment and the 3rd Sikhs. The 4th Brigade had meanwhile followed up, and the 36th Sikhs, covered by long-range volleys from the K.O.S.B.'s and by the fire of two guns of No. 1 Mountain Battery, Royal Artillery, seized a ridge beyond the first one over which the pass goes.

As the 2nd Brigade were seen by Brigadier-General Spraggs to be nearing the crest which was first seized, he sent on No. 5 Bombay Mountain Battery to a still more advanced position than that occupied by the 2nd Division batteries, to help clear the surrounding heights.

Captain De Butts, R.A., was commanding this battery, and as he was turning a corner to look for a good position in which to bring his guns into action, a shot hit him in the stomach and he died a very few minutes afterwards. This officer was a great loss to the force; he had taken part in the Suakim Campaign, had been invalided from there, and only just rejoined his battery in time to take part in the Tirah Expedition.

Two guns of this battery, however, and two guns of No. 9 Mountain Battery, Royal Artillery, were able to find sufficient room to come into action, and shelled the enemy in the few remaining sangars they were occupying.

By 11.30 A.M. all firing was over, and the enemy were streaming away into the Mastura Valley, setting fire, as they went, to the stacks of fodder near some of the houses below the pass. Our casualties were about twenty-four: the Queen's having one killed and seven wounded, and the Yorkshire Regiment, No. 8 Mountain Battery, Royal Artillery, the 2nd Battalion 4th Ghoorkhas, and the 36th Sikhs making up the remaining casualties.

The feebleness of the opposition offered was most unexpected. Every one in India seemed to have imagined that a great stand would be made at the Sampagha Pass by Orakzais and Afridis combined; and the fact that it was not so is very probably due to the way in which they had been turned out of a position at Dargai far more impregnable, and by only a moiety of the force brought into array against them on the Sampagha.

No sooner had the position on the Sampagha been taken than the troops were pushed on into the Mastura Valley. We had all heard a good deal of the fertility of Tirah; but I think I may say that, despite this, every one was astonished at the appearance it presented. Well watered, highly cultivated, comparatively speaking flat and open, with massively-built homesteads surrounded by fruit trees, and with large stacks of fodder in the courtyards or on the mud roofs, and with numerous trees dotting the steep sides of the valley—it seemed quite like a Garden of Eden in comparison with the barren, inhospitable country which is generally so characteristic of the North-West Frontier.

It was clearly impossible to fight an action and push two whole divisions with their transport over an unmade road into the Mastura Valley in the one day, more particularly as the ascent to the pass from Karappa Camp involved a climb of about 3,000 feet or more, the summit of the pass being nearly 7,000 feet high, and the descent to the Mastura Valley being about 1,000 feet. Orders were therefore given for Brigadier-General Hart's Brigade, the three regiments of which, though they had done but little fighting, had so materially assisted in the success of the second and fourth brigades, to remain on the Sampagha Pass for the night, and to protect the transport animals and baggage. Every effort was made to get the mules carrying the great-coats and blankets up to the corps ahead. This, however, could only be managed in a very few instances, and most officers and regiments had to spend a bitterly cold night without these necessities. None of the baggage belonging to Major-General Yeatman-Biggs and his staff reached camp that night, and many an improvident British soldier, who had eaten his day's supply of food earlier in the day, owed what he got that night to the generosity of the more frugal Sikhs and Ghoorkhas. The latter willingly shared their chupatties or unleavened cakes with hungry members of British regiments in the same brigade, despite the fact that, however famished they might have been themselves, they would not, as Hindoos, have been able to accept any similar cooked food from the hand of a Christian.

The 2nd Division, with the 2nd Brigade and divisional troops of the 1st Division, had to spend the whole of the next day in the Mastura Valley, for it was only by one corps borrowing supplies from another, by distributing all that came over the pass, and by foraging for grain in the surrounding villages, that two days' rations per man could be issued.

It was at the same time most important to advance and attack the Arhanga Pass before the tribesmen had time to recover from the defeat they had experienced on the Sampagha, and before they had leisure to burn, hide or remove their grain and fodder. Sir William Lockhart and staff accompanied a reconnaissance made during the day towards the Arhanga Pass, and the plan of attack was decided on. The order for the advance next day was for the 4th Brigade (Brigadier-General Westmacott's) to lead, followed by the 3rd and then the 2nd, the baggage following in rear of the column.

Tremendous efforts had been made by Brigadier-General **Hart, C.B., V.C.,** by Colonel Christopher, commissary-general, and by all the commissariat and transport officers, to get the baggage and supplies forward; and the sapper and miner companies had worked unceasingly at improving the road. It was solely owing to this that the troops moving on to the attack of the Arhanga were again completed with their transport animals and supplies.

The 4th Brigade moved with the K.O.S.B.'s leading, and seized a long conical hill opposite to and broadways on to the centre of the pass, and on this the three batteries of the 2nd Division, under Lieutenant-Colonel Purdy, came into action.

The 3rd Brigade moved off to the left; and the

4th Brigade advanced against the centre, while the 2nd Brigade, accompanied by Major-General Symons, made an attack on a high hill which commands the pass on the enemy's left flank. To all intents and purposes this latter brigade took the position by itself, for the enemy made practically no resistance; and when the Yorkshire Regiment and 2nd Battalion 4th Ghoorkhas, who raced for the top of the hill, had crowned the crest (the Yorkshire Regiment just arriving first), the enemy, of whom there were not very many visible, evacuated the position entirely, and the troops at once continued their march into Afridi Tirah.

The ascent to the Arhanga Pass was still more difficult than that to the Sampagha; and the sappers and miners at once set to work to improve the road on both sides. Such was their success that by dark a very large proportion of the most necessary transports, such as greatcoats and blankets, had arrived in camp at Maidan, the new camping ground selected. The casualties in this attack were only two, one of them being Captain Searle, 36th Sikhs, who was severely wounded.

Having reached the heart of Tirah, it seemed to many people that the campaign was now practically over; that Afridis and Orakzais would make haste to comply with our terms and get us out of their country; and that, in fact, everything was over except the shouting. These views were in a great measure correct as regards the Orakzais; but the Afridis held quite a different opinion, as events from the night of the 31st October most clearly showed.

CHAPTER IX.

DESCRIPTION OF AFRIDI TIRAH. THE AFRIDI'S GUERILLA TACTICS.

THE force was now in the centre of the Maidan Valley, the most fertile and important portion of country in all Afridi Tirah, which had never before been visited by an invading army, British or otherwise, or, as far as I know, by a single European.

The country had, of course, never been surveyed, and on the maps supplied to the force Afridi Tirah was more or less a blank, though the direction of the main streams had been dotted in—a conventional sign in topography to indicate that their position is not really known, and that the direction they are shown as taking is supposititious and derived in all probability from information supplied by natives who have reported on the country. The position even of the Arhanga Pass was very erroneously marked on the maps, being shown far too much to the west; but although the actual position of the streams watering the Maidan Valley was of course not correct, it was nevertheless wonderful how accurately on the whole their general direction had been depicted; and the maps were far from being useless even when we reached a totally unsurveyed country.

From native information it was supposed that a large portion of Tirah was covered with forests of pine trees; and one had pictured the blazing camp fires which could be made at night by the help of the resinous wood. The northern slopes of the ranges of hills in which the Arhanga Pass is situated were, it is true, dotted fairly thickly with trees, and here and there they were sufficiently numerous to make a small wood or copse; but there was certainly nothing in the way of a forest in the whole of Tirah.

Maidan, the summer home of the Afridis, where the main column was now encamped, is a large valley about twelve miles long by six miles wide, surrounded on all sides by mountains.

The average height of the valley itself may be said to be about 6,000 feet, and that of the ranges of hills which surround it about 7,000 feet, though considerably higher in places. In the north-west corner there is a gap which allows the streams which water the Maidan Valley to emerge into the Dwatoi Valley; and here the hills are of less altitude.

The Sher Darra is the first stream one encounters on entering Maidan. Its general direction is west, and, as always happens in mountainous country, the main river is joined by numerous affluents, most of them dry, except in the rains. When it nears the range of mountains on the west (an offshoot from the Safed Koh, or white mountain), it gradually turns north, and receives still more affluents; finally, at Bagh, in the north-west corner of the valley, it has been joined by so many other streams or watercourses that it becomes the Sholaba, or twenty waters.

The Sholaba then flows north of the range of hills which forms the northern boundary of the Tirah Valley, down the difficult Sholaba or Dwatoi defile, till it reaches Dwatoi (or two streams), and there joins the Rajgul stream, where the two combined form the Bara River, which flows down to Bara close to Peshawur. It was by this Sholaba and Bara Valley, that the second division moved from Bagh to the camp on the Bara River, near Peshawur, in the early part of December, when Tirah was being evacuated to avoid the snowfall, the time for which had nearly come.

When one talks of a valley, people who have not been in India, especially in the northern part of it, probably picture to themselves a valley such as one sees in England, with the meadows gently sloping down to the river which flows peacefully along in the centre. The valleys among the mountains of Tirah are not, unfortunately, of this nature. Had they been so the protection of the camp would have been a very easy matter.

From the mountain ranges on all four sides of the Maidan Valley numerous spurs jut out, and between these spurs there are, of course, small valleys. The sides of these spurs are so steep, and the character of the soil is so rocky, that when rain falls, as it sometimes does very heavily in the monsoon or rainy season, the water pours off the spurs on either side, for the soil, which is very scanty on the mountain sides, absorbs but little. This water digs for itself deep watercourses or nullahs, and, rushing headlong down, tears away the banks till they stand perpendicularly or even jut over in places. All these watercourses or nullahs eventually contribute their quota of water to the main stream, which, though in dry weather but a few inches deep, is a running torrent in heavy rains.

The whole valley is a series of sloping plateaux formed by the prolongation of the spurs, some small and some large, but all gradually sloping down towards the main stream and with their ends and sides steeply scarped by the rushing water at the time of the annual rains. To prevent the water flowing off the slopes at the lower ends of these spurs, where there is a sufficient amount of earth to permit of cultivation, the ground has been made into a series of terraces, with a steep bank from two to three feet high between each; instead, therefore, of the water rushing away at once, it has time to soak into the soil, thereby fertilizing it for the planting of crops.

The above system of cultivation is adopted in all hilly or mountainous districts of India; but, whereas in the Himalayas soil is scarce and the ground is full of stones and boulders, which are taken out of the ground as far as may be and piled up to form retaining walls to the terraces, in Tirah, on the other hand, the soil is so rich and plentiful on the lower slopes of the spurs, that the banks are in most cases of earth, and the soil is much richer than on the slopes of the Punjaub hills.

The whole valley, therefore, consists of a series of these terraced plateaux, with a deep nullah or watercourse on each side; and Camp Maidan, as it was called, was on an especially large terraced plateau, with the main stream on the one side and a watercourse leading into the main stream on two other sides. A few hundred yards apart on each terraced plateau are two or more well-built homesteads surrounded by outbuildings. As a rule, in the upper or eastern portion of the Maidan Valley only one house is built on each little plateau, though on the very large plateau or series of plateaux on which the camp was situated there were, of course, several of such edifices. Further down the valley, however, in the direction of Bagh and west of Maidan camp, the buildings are far more

Description of Afridi Tirah.

numerous, though not, as a rule, so large, or covering such an extent of ground, as those further east. It would almost appear as if the eastern portion of the valley was inhabited by rich landowners, whereas the smaller peasant proprietors lived further to the west.

The Zakka Khels, by far the most powerful tribe among the Afridis, and our most formidable and inveterate foes, inhabit the eastern portion of the valley through which leads the principal road and pass into the winter settlements in the Bara and Bazar valleys. This tribe takes toll of all the other tribes when they, with their wives, families, and flocks, are on the move between their summer houses in Tirah and their winter settlements nearer Peshawur; and it is, perhaps, on this account that the Zakka Khel tribe especially have such large and commodious homesteads.

Of all the Pathan tribes which inhabit the north-west border and attempt to steal rifles from Peshawur, Rawal Pindi, and other cantonments, the Zakka Khels are the most daring and skilful; so little are they to be trusted that native regiments who enlist Afridis are very loth to take Zakka Khels, more especially the regiments serving on or near the frontier, where a man can desert with his rifle and be over the border the same night.

The homesteads I have spoken of, both in the Mastura valley and in Afridi Tirah, are large, commodious, two or three storeyed houses, built of mud and timber, the timber being used not only for rafters, but as supports in the walls themselves. The principal living rooms appear, as a rule, to be on the first floor, the ground floor being used as a store room for Indian corn, potatoes, grain, &c., and the upper storey partly as living rooms and partly as store rooms. The roofs are all flat, and the outhouses, which are also very solidly built and with flat roofs, are probably most of them used as cattle sheds; when the expedition arrived, however, the cattle had been driven off and the outhouses were either empty or crammed inside and on the roof with Indian corn, of which there were also large stacks on the ground.

It was on the stalks of the Indian corn that the transport animals were chiefly fed, the grain serving as oats, and the stalks as hay; but near some houses were also stacks of grass which the horses, at all events, preferred to the Indian corn.

A considerable number of fowls were found in and round each house when we arrived in the Mastura and Maidan valleys, and, needless to say, they were very quickly caught and cooked. Cats and dogs were also found in great numbers. One would imagine that the latter would have followed their owners when they moved out of the valley, but the Afridi dog seems to resemble the cat of every country, in that it is more attached to the house than to the owner. In houses where the owners had been rather taken aback by our sudden advance from the Mastura valley, were found pots of honey, dried apricots, walnuts, jars full of flour, and all sorts of little seeds in packets, probably intended for the spring sowing; and in every house, in addition to the Indian corn, there were pumpkins and large quantities of red beans, called in Egypt lubiya or lobiya. These latter require an immense amount of cooking and boiling before they are really tender. As vegetables of any kind had been scarce since leaving Kohat, they were at first very acceptable, but after a very short time one got extremely tired of them, so tasteless and indigestible did they prove.

The Afridis had doubtless carried off very large quantities of grain, as distinguished from forage, and as we descended into the Maidan valley on the evening of the 31st, many tribesmen, with their women, children, and flocks of cattle and laden animals, could be seen ascending the hills on the far side. The whole valley was, of course, quite impracticable for cavalry, who would have been obliged to keep to a path and move in single file; and the fact of not being able to use cavalry to pursue a beaten foe enables the tribesmen, secure of their retreat, to hold on to a position much more confidently than they would otherwise do. In the evenings the women and cattle could be seen again descending the hills to reach houses and stacks of fodder hitherto untouched by us and out of the near reach of the camp, and they doubtless in the early mornings removed a good deal of grain into the mountains above.

A very large quantity of grain had been buried either in the houses or in the ground, and in the latter case the newly-turned earth was generally concealed by burning forage and Indian corn stalks, not only over the place where the grain had been buried but in a good many other spots, in the hope we should lose our time in digging in the wrong places and thus give up the search. Ghoorkhas and Sikhs, however, were not easily baffled by tricks of this sort, with which they are well acquainted, and large quantities were dug up every day, though no doubt a good deal that was buried further away from houses escaped detection.

Round each house were numerous fruit trees—apple, walnut, peach, apricot and fig-trees especially—and altogether both Afridis and Orakzais appeared to make themselves considerably more comfortable than most natives of India do. The principal crops, though they had all unfortunately been gathered long before we arrived, were Indian corn, wheat, rice, potatoes and turnips, and the red beans I have alluded to before.

I omitted to say, in speaking of the houses, that nearly every considerable one had a loopholed tower for defensive purposes against tribal raids; or, if there was no tower, the upper rooms and top storeys of the house would be loopholed. These towers, or the roofs themselves, allow the tribesman when time is hanging heavily on his hands, to take shots at his enemy entering or leaving the next house, and with the minimum amount of danger to himself.

It is now time to return to a description of the highly-successful guerilla warfare which, from the night of the 31st October, the tribesmen, and more especially the Zakka Khels, conducted against us.

Perhaps because we had taken the Arhanga Pass with so little difficulty, and it was imagined that the road to the camp at Maidan would now be safe, or perhaps owing to the confusion of the forward movement, a convoy was allowed to proceed from the Arhanga Pass in the dusk on the very evening we had captured it. The convoy was principally escorted by the 15th Sikhs, and as is natural with transport animals on a bad and unmade road, some moved faster and some slower, so that the distance from the head to the tail of the convoy was considerable.

This was the opportunity the Afridis had been waiting for—a large number of defenceless mule drivers, with an escort scattered here and there, moving along a strange path and in the dark, so that the escort would not see to shoot. They swooped down from all sides on the Sikh escort, who, unable to protect the whole of such a long and straggling line, very wisely determined that at all events they would lose none of the mules carrying ammunition, and especially rallied round these; but in the confusion, inseparable from such attacks, some sixty other mules broke away, carrying 200 kits, which of course fell into the enemy's hands, nine drivers also were killed and wounded.

This was most unfortunate, but what happened the next night was still more so, for, emboldened by the success of the first night, a large number of tribesmen placed themselves on the flat roofs of some houses close underneath which another convoy was passing in the dark, and jumped from thence into the middle of the drivers and animals moving below, whilst other tribesmen attacked from all sides. On this occasion another sixty mules got away with some 350 kits, ten boxes of Lee-Metford ammunition, a treasure chest, with fortunately but little in it, and some rifles; three men of the 2nd Queen's Regiment were killed and four wounded.

The loss and confusion would have been very much greater but for the extremely gallant conduct of a lance-corporal in the Queen's Regiment named Simpson. This Regiment was holding the Arhanga Pass that night, and as a good many of the Queen's were on escort duty with the convoy, their officers, as it proceeded over the pass on its way to Maidan Camp, cautioned the non-commissioned officers and men of the escort to keep together in groups, and not move singly.

Lance-Corporal Simpson more especially laid these instructions to heart, for he collected thirteen men, and moved with fixed bayonets. As the convoy passed, some of the Pathans dropped off the roof and began cutting up the mule-drivers; others made a sudden attack on Lance-Corporal Simpson's party, hoping to catch them unawares; but, so far from doing this, were bayoneted and shot down. This young non-commissioned officer then took his men a little up the hillside and fired volleys at the Pathans who were on or near the house whence the attack had been made. The tribesmen tried to get above Lance-Corporal Simpson and his party, but he again moved his men still further up the hillside and fired steady volleys —so steady that an officer of the Northampton Regiment, who was with the rearguard to the convoy, said that they were as regular as if they had been fired on an inspection parade.

It is improbable that the physical damage done by this firing in the dark was very great, but the moral effect was enormous, for it kept other men in good heart, made the tribesmen imagine they were dealing with a much larger body of men than was really the case, and greatly tended to lessen the general confusion inseparable from an attack on a convoy in the dark.

It now became clear that the Afridis were bent on doing all the mischief they could to detached parties, etc.; and orders were issued forbidding the movement of any transport along the road after a certain hour, a precaution which made the movement of convoys from the 2nd November onwards very much safer than before; and as time went on, the road leading up to the Arhanga Pass, from Camp Mastura and down over the pass into the Maidan Camp, was extremely well guarded by strongly entrenched pickets posted on various hills above the road.

With the exception of the reconnaissance made to the Saran Sar Pass on the 9th November, and of the retirement from Warán on the 16th, on both of which occasions there were heavy casualties, the losses suffered by the troops in Maidan Camp occurred chiefly when out foraging, and also to a certain extent from the shooting into camp at night.

On the 6th November, Lieutenant Giffard, of the Northampton Regiment, was shot dead while sitting at dinner about 7 p.m., and the same afternoon about 4 p.m., Captain Sullivan, of the 36th Sikhs, who had just hurried out from England to rejoin his regiment, and had only arrived in camp about an hour before, was hit by a stray bullet through the arm and had to be invalided at once. On the night of the 8th November, Captain Watson, of the Commissariat Department, was walking about in camp before dinner, when a bullet—I believe the only one fired into camp that evening—hit him through the head, and death was almost instantaneous. On the night when Lieutenant Giffard was killed and Captain Sullivan wounded, there were, as far as I can remember, no casualties amongst the rank and file of either British or native troops or amongst followers.

It seems a remarkable fatality that the only three bullets which so unfortunately did harm, all hit British officers, for, in the vast crowd of men and followers, more especially as it was either dusk or nearly so, they could not possibly have been designedly aimed at.

Hardly a day passed in the early part of November but that some casualties occurred when the foraging parties were returning, for the tribesmen, who offered little or no resistance to the advance of the party, always pressed heavily on the retirement.

On the 9th November the Dorsetshire Regiment lost one man killed and nine wounded in returning from foraging. Another day the enemy very skilfully worked round in rear of the covering party and drove off forty mules; and when the retirement took place the mule carrying the axle of a mountain gun was shot, and the axle had to be abandoned, a mishap which, until another axle could be procured from the arsenal, left the battery with only five guns.

On the 10th November Lieutenant Cameron, of the Gordon Highlanders, was wounded by a long shot while on foraging duty; Lieutenant Caffin, of the Yorkshire Regiment, was wounded on the same duty another day, and in a reconnaissance made to Bagh, Captain MacLaren, of the K.O.S.B., was slightly wounded. Not a day passed but that some men or followers were killed or wounded by these wonderfully skilled marksmen, who are extremely difficult to see at all times, so expert are they in taking cover; and when, as was so frequently the case, they fired from long ranges with Lee-Metford rifles and smokeless powder, there was no smoke discernible to indicate even their approximate position.

These constant losses were very disheartening, but it is extremely difficult to see how they could

Description of Afridi Tirah.

have been avoided. Forage and grain must be obtained, village towers from whence the camp has been fired on must be destroyed, and though skilful skirmishers who are covering the retirement may minimize the losses and occasionally escape them entirely by never grouping together, and thus never offering a target to the enemy, still, once a man is killed or wounded, he must be carried by three or four of his comrades, and then, with the increased target offered, further losses occurred.

As regards the firing into camp too, although all the hills around were very carefully picketed at night, and the Ghoorkha scouts did excellent service in "stalking the stalker," the tribesmen nevertheless changed their ground every evening, and it was impossible to say where the fire might come from; moreover, a good many of the shots were fired at random into the camp from very long ranges.

All the outposts in the world could not have prevented this, and though a good many letters were written to the papers saying that this or that should not have happened, no means were suggested by which the occurrences could be prevented.

As long as the tribesmen are as well armed as they are now, and as long as they are such skilful marksmen, with abundant ammunition, and a thorough acquaintance with the country, so long will troops operating against them suffer from well-directed fire at long ranges, and be fired into at night, without being able to bring their foes to bay.

CHAPTER X.

EVENTS IN CAMP MAIDAN, AND THE ACTIONS ON THE 9TH AND 16TH NOVEMBER.

WHILE the troops at Maidan were engaged in foraging, and the commissariat and transport department were busily occupied in bringing up supplies, tents, and heavy baggage from Shinawari—and while Sir Thomas Holdich, R.E., and the survey department were taking every opportunity of surveying the country—the political officers with the force were by no means idle.

The moment we were settled in Maidan steps were taken to inform the various sections of the Afridi and Orakzai tribes that, if they would send in their jirgahs, or deputations, the terms of the Government would be made known to them.

The Orakzais of the Samal faction had been ready from the first to make terms, but it seemed for some days as if the other section, the Gar, would not follow their example. On the 11th of

November, however, the Gar-Orakzai jirgahs also arrived, and as the Afridis (and more especially the Zakka Khels, who had sent in an insulting message) showed no signs of sending in their jirgahs, Sir William Lockhart decided that the terms demanded from the Orakzais should be made known to their representatives without waiting for the Afridis.

The men of the jirgahs, mostly old greybeards and numbering about 100 in all, had been fed and housed just outside the camp. On the 12th of November they were brought in and interviewed by Sir William Lockhart, who conveyed to them, through Sir Richard Udny (the chief political officer and a very fine Pushtu scholar), the terms imposed by the Indian Government.

These conditions were, that all Government property in their hands, taken either from the Khyber or other forts, should be restored, that a fine of 30,000 rupees should be paid, and that 500 breech-loading rifles should be handed in, whilst all subsidies hitherto granted would be forfeited. And to comply with these terms they were allowed fourteen days.

Although the Orakzai jirgahs remained absolutely impassive as the terms were being explained to them, it is known that they were very much relieved to hear that their country would not be annexed, and that they returned to their homes with considerably lighter hearts than they had set out.

The Orakzais appear to have been in some little doubt at first as to how to divide the indemnity which they would have to pay, between the Samal and Gar factions, the origin of which I have explained in the first chapter; and while they were divided on this point, the resistance previously offered to foraging parties and the damage done at night by cutting the telegraph wire continued.

Brigadier-General Hart's brigade (the 1st), which had remained in the Mastura valley as a reminder to the Orakzais that their villages were at our mercy, had made itself extremely secure in camp by strong pickets on the surrounding hills, and sent out foraging parties to the adjoining villages in the same way as was being done in Maidan.

On the 13th November Brigadier-General Hart

sent out a foraging party composed of one squadron 18th Bengal Lancers and five companies of infantry from different corps. The enemy attacked in force, and Major G. Money, 18th Bengal Lancers, was slightly wounded, and Captain Bowman, Derbyshire Regiment, severely so. The troops were most admirably handled by Major Smith-Dorrien, D.S.O., of the Derbyshire Regiment, and the enemy were repulsed with loss. After this a battery was sent to strengthen No. 1 Brigade, and Mr. Donald, the political officer specially accredited to the Orakzais, went to Mastura to ascertain the cause of this attack made while negotiations were proceeding.

Great pains had been taken to ensure, both in the Mastura and in the Maidan valley, that if foraging parties were not fired on from the houses, the fortified towers and buildings should be spared; for if any section of a tribe declined to accede to the terms, the threat of destroying such property would very possibly bring them to their senses.

Three Afridi tribes had sent in their jirgahs on the 9th November, and three more had promised to do so; but the Zakka Khels, inhabiting the eastern portion of the valley and the range over which the Saran Sar pass leads, continued obdurate. To them, also, was to be attributed the constant interference with the telegraph, which was cut every night: the poles also, and on one occasion nearly a mile of wire, were removed. The Zakka Khels, indeed, were principally responsible for the attacks on convoys, the firing into camp, and the shooting from long ranges at the foraging parties, whilst it was well known that they were the prime instigators of, and participators in, the attack on the Khyber.

The Saran Sar is the principal egress from Maidan into the Bara and Bazar valleys, and it was down this pass that the tribesmen with their women and cattle could be seen descending every night to reach the homesteads below it. It was, therefore, determined to make a reconnaissance to the top of this pass, fix its position on the map, and destroy some of the Zakka Khel towers. General Westmacott with a mixed brigade was selected for this duty, the troops being the Dorsetshire and Northamptonshire Regiments, the 15th and 36th Sikhs, No. 4 Company Madras

Sappers and Miners, and two Mountain Batteries, No. 8 British and No. 5 Bombay.

There is a conical hill at the foot of the main slope up which the path winds to the pass, and in the western side of this conical hill is a nullah or deep dry watercourse, which, with many twists and turns, runs right up to the camp, near which it joins the main stream. This nullah is the ravine in which nearly all the Northampton's losses occurred later in the day; it has steep precipitous banks, and once in the bottom of the nullah, it is not always easy to find a sloping bank by which to climb out.

There was some little opposition as the troops neared the hill, and the plan of attack consisted in the Northampton Regiment making a direct advance up the hill supported by the 36th Sikhs, the 15th Sikhs remaining with the guns, and the Dorsetshire Regiment advancing against the enemy's right flank up a ravine which forms the source of the nullah previously described.

If the enemy had elected to hold on to the position, the flank attack would have taken them on their right flank and rear. They made little or no real resistance, however, though a smart fire was opened on the Northamptonshire Regiment when they were about half-way up the hill; but the infantry, assisted by the fire of two batteries, quickly gained the crest, and before the flank attack had time to develop. The Dorsetshire Regiment had been a good deal fired on as they advanced up the ravine, and met with five casualties; but no losses were incurred in the frontal attack.

It was now about 11 A.M., and Sir William Lockhart and staff arrived somewhat later. Everything in the way of surveying and reconnaissance having been effected, the retirement began about 2.15 P.M. The orders for the homeward movement were for the 36th Sikhs (three companies) to hold the saddle or neck over which the road passes, until the main body of the Northampton Regiment, who were on a peak further to the south-east, had retired on to them. The Sikhs were then to retire to the foot of the hill, the main body of the Northampton Regiment covering the retirement of their own rear companies.

The Dorsetshire Regiment, in descending the hill

and also on reaching the foot, were to protect the right flank of the retiring column, assisted by a company of the 15th Sikhs, while some of the 36th Sikhs covered the other flank.

Directly the retirement began, the enemy, hitherto invisible, reappeared like magic in very large numbers, and one man of the Northamptons was killed and seven wounded almost immediately. The ground was much too steep and rocky to permit of the use of stretchers, and the dead and wounded had to be carried over this precipitous ground, a work of immense difficulty, which could not be accomplished except by four men carrying a wounded comrade and a fifth holding the five rifles, in addition to his own. This took up a very large number out of one company, and the retirement proceeded but slowly.

The 36th Sikhs (three companies), who, in accordance with their orders, had gone down to the bottom of the hill when relieved, were again sent up it, under Lieutenant-Colonel Haughton, to relieve some of the pressure on the Northamptons.

Finally, about 5 P.M., all the Northampton

Regiment were down the hill, and by 5.30 P.M. the three companies of the 36th Sikhs, through whom they had passed. When the whole of the Northamptons had descended and the head of the regiment had commenced the homeward march, the rearmost battery was ordered to join the one further on nearer the camp; and when all the wounded were reported safe, the two batteries were sent on to camp with an escort of the Sappers and Miners, the growing darkness no longer permitting them to fire.

Lieutenant-Colonel Haughton, commanding the 36th Sikhs, who had covered the withdrawal of the Northampton Regiment down the lower portion of the slope, began his own retirement round the eastern side of the conical hill which the battery had reached.

Hardly had he begun the movement, however, than he heard firing from the western or other end of the hill, near the place where the Northampton Regiment had been seen to enter a ravine on commencing their retirement. Thereupon he halted his regiment, and sent to ascertain the cause of the firing. He received a report that the Northampton Regiment were all clear away, but as some of the enemy could be seen making down the hill in the direction of the ravine into which they had entered, several volleys were fired at them.

It was now getting dark, and an officer of the Northampton Regiment, who brought up some wounded men to where Brigadier-General Westmacott and his staff were standing, reported that all the wounded were up; the General therefore, who could see the 36th Sikhs still occupying the conical hill, ordered the "retire" to be sounded. The remainder of the brigade then halted until the 36th Sikhs had got into line on the flank; and after a short time the retirement was again commenced, with the Dorsets guarding the right flank and the 36th Sikhs on the left.

It must be clearly understood that the ground at the foot of the hill was by no means a plain with the one nullah running through it; on the contrary, it was very much broken and intersected, and although by day communication between regiments advancing on such ground can be maintained by signal, once it is dark no further command or supervision can be exercised. As a matter of fact it was in returning to camp in the dusk that all or nearly all our losses occurred.

It was no doubt most unfortunate, as it turned out, that the Northampton Regiment should have entered the nullah at all; or that, having done so, exceptionally strong flanking parties were not kept out, for as soon as night begins to fall in country like Tirah, each regiment must entirely look after its own safety. The comparatively level, though stony bed of the nullah no doubt rendered the transport of the dead and wounded much easier than the rough and broken ground above would have done, but the constant turns and twists of the ravine made communication between the head and tail of the regiment most difficult, if not impossible.

The leading company had almost reached camp when the rear of the column was desperately assaulted by a large number of tribesmen, who had descended from the hill and followed up in the dusk as soon as they saw the Northampton Regiment, encumbered as they were with wounded, enter the nullah. Desperate fighting ensued in the dark, the Afridis from the precipitous banks above firing into the men carrying the dead and wounded below; and for some time at all events a large number of the regiment were taken at an enormous disadvantage.

Officers and men fought undauntedly against overwhelming odds, and stood by their wounded. At a critical moment a detached company of the 36th Sikhs under Lieutenant Van Someren, together with some of the Dorset Regiment, appeared to the assistance of the sorely pressed companies in the nullah, and drove the enemy off; both the Dorsets and the 36th Sikhs then assisted in conveying the now numerous killed and wounded back to camp. Such was the disastrous ending, as far as the Northampton Regiment was concerned, to a reconnaissance which, owing to Brigadier-General Westmacott's excellent dispositions, had been a brilliant success till darkness came on.

There is no doubt but that the officers and men of the Northampton Regiment who were engaged in escorting the dead and wounded behaved magnificently. All the stretchers were full when Lieutenant Trent was hit in the thigh with a Lee-

Metford bullet. One of the wounded men in a stretcher said he could manage to walk, and thus enabled Lieutenant Trent to be carried. The party carrying him and the other wounded were now left without a single man to return the enemy's fire; all were engaged in carrying dead and wounded. At a critical juncture Lieutenant Trent's stretcher broke, but the men carrying it coolly repaired it under a heavy fire, two of them being shot through the clothes as they did so. Lieutenant Macintyre, a sergeant, and eleven men were the last of all, and they were urged to retire; but this officer said he could not leave the wounded, and all twelve died in trying to defend them, their bodies were found next day in the nullah.

The casualties in this affair were:—

Northamptonshire Regiment.—Lieutenants Waddell and Macintyre and nineteen men killed, and Lieutenant Trent and twenty-nine men wounded.

Dorsetshire Regiment.—Lieutenants Ingham and Mercer and six men wounded.

15th Sikhs.—Two killed and two wounded.

36th Sikhs.—Four wounded.

It is impossible to estimate the enemy's losses,

but a very large number of the Zakka Khel towers were destroyed, and huge quantities of forage were brought into camp by foraging parties who went out that day, with a loss of two men killed and four wounded.

The previous day a determined attack had been made on a convoy before it reached the Arhanga Pass, on the way from Mastura to Maidan; but Brigadier-General Hart had despatched the 2nd Battalion 1st Ghoorkhas of his brigade to co-operate with the Yorkshire Regiment (19th), who were holding the pass; and the enemy lost twenty men killed (twelve of their rifles being captured) and a good many wounded—a success to which the Ghoorkha scouts largely contributed.

On the 11th another reconnaissance to the Saran Sar was conducted up to and even beyond the point reached two days previously. Brigadier-General Gaselee had charge of the operations, which were a complete success, the troops under him being the Queen's, the Yorkshire Regiment, the 24th Ghoorkhas, the 3rd Sikhs, the 13th Ghoorkhas, with two batteries.

Sir William Lockhart again accompanied the

reconnaissance; but the retirement was ordered to begin not later than 12 noon, and the troops were back in camp by 4.30 P.M. On the 9th the retirement had begun at 2 P.M., or even a little later, and camp had been reached at 6.45 P.M., so that in both cases it occupied about the same time; but the troops under Brigadier-General Gaselee had the great advantage of daylight during the whole movement. The retirement in both cases was conducted very slowly and steadily down the hill, the artillery keeping the enemy back whenever they showed themselves in groups; and as the distance from the Saran Sar to camp is about four and a half miles, this gives a rate of retirement of about one mile an hour.

Under cover of this reconnaissance, Brigadier-General Kempster's brigade foraged on a very large scale, and the remaining fortified towers and posts belonging to the Zakka Khels were destroyed, including a place called Chikkun, where one of the principal Zakka Khel chiefs lived. On this occasion Lieutenant Wright (2nd Queen's) was slightly wounded, and one man was killed and one wounded. The casualties, owing to Brigadier-

General Gaselee's skilful dispositions, and the steady way in which the retirement was conducted, were therefore trifling, and Sir William Lockhart, in orders, conveyed his entire appreciation of the day's work.

During the 9th November three Afridi tribes had sent in their jirgahs, and on the 12th the Orakzais had practically announced their intention of accepting the terms; for they asked the political officers to apportion between the Gar and Samal factions the amount of the indemnity demanded. The Aka Khel Afridis inhabiting the Warān valley had also announced their desire to be on friendly terms, and on the 13th the experiment was tried of buying grain from the Malikdin and Kambar Khel tribesmen, whose jirgahs had come in.

Altogether the political situation looked much more promising, and the firing into camp at night had very greatly diminished, though the Zakka Khels still continued actively hostile.

A section of this tribe inhabits Warān, and an expedition under Brigadier-General Kempster, consisting of his own brigade, and strengthened by the 36th Sikhs, No. 5 Bombay and No. 8

British Mountain Batteries, with No. 4 Madras and No. 4 Bombay Sapper and Miner Companies, started on the 13th to visit Warān by the Tseri pass leading into it from Maidan. The Aka Khels, the principal inhabitants, continued friendly, and neither was the movement over the pass interfered with, nor was the camp fired into on arrival. Moreover, forage in large quantities was obtained without opposition, and everything appeared quiet.

This was no doubt largely due to the influence possessed over the Afridi tribes by Colonel Warburton, for many years political resident in the Khyber, who accompanied Brigadier-General Kempster's force. He had retired from the service before the Afridi outbreak took place, and the Government of India, aware of the influence he possessed over the tribesmen, induced him to return and accompany the expedition as one of the political officers.

Up till the 14th all was quiet in Warān, and in the Mastura and Maidan valleys, but on the 15th the situation in Warān seems to have changed.

The previous day a reconnaissance had been made towards the south-east end of the valley in which stands or stood the house of Saiad Akbar, who is one of, if not the principal, Afridi mullah or priest, and who had been most active in persuading the tribesmen to take up arms against the Indian Government. His house was very strongly built and fortified, and was blown up by the Sappers and Miners, great care being taken not to injure the adjoining mosque.

On the 15th a reconnaissance was pushed out to the point where the Warān and Mastura valleys join, due military precautions being taken as on the 13th and 14th. The wisdom of this course was soon exemplified, for some tribesmen were seen rifle in hand, and a flag of truce was sent towards them. This they immediately fired on, killing one man and wounding another; and they continued to fire both during the outward and homeward march, and also into camp at night, seven more casualties resulting.

Colonel Warburton now received information that the Zakka Khels had entered Warān on the night of the 14th, and had tried to incite the

Aka Khels to fight. When they found the latter were unwilling to do so, they fired on us and on the flag of truce (a symbol with which they are perfectly acquainted and use themselves) in the hope that we, thinking they were Aka Khels, would retaliate by burning and blowing up Aka Khel fortified villages and houses. The interference of the Zakka Khels was, however, suspected, and no damage was consequently done to the Aka Khel buildings.

Orders had been received for Brigadier-General Kempster to return to Maidan on the 16th. The firing into camp was very hot on the night of the 15th, and several star shells were fired, but there were fortunately no casualties on our side.

The movement back to Maidan camp began early on the 16th; the baggage and transport animals being sent on well ahead. The 15th Sikhs were to hold the pass, and Colonel Travers commanded the rearguard, which consisted of his own regiment (the 1st Battalion 2nd Ghoorkhas), a company of the Gordon Highlanders, a company of the Dorsetshire Regiment (who had been holding hills above the camp), the 3rd Ghoorkha scouts and No. 8 British Mountain Battery.

This force began to move off about 9 A.M., and for some time all went well, the enemy only shooting from very long distances. The two companies of Sappers and Miners had greatly improved the road over the pass, but even so the transport moved but slowly, and between 12 noon and 1 P.M. Colonel Travers held on to a position to enable the main body to increase its distance.

It was when the rearguard began to move again that the enemy commenced to press the retirement, more especially on the left flank; and three Ghoorkhas were killed and five wounded. To these, Surgeon Captain Selby, the medical officer attached to the 1st Battalion 3rd Ghoorkhas, attended with the greatest coolness under a heavy fire, binding up their wounds as unconcernedly as if he had been in his hospital in cantonments.

The rearguard reached the pass held by the 15th Sikhs just about 3 P.M., greatly exhausted by the very difficult work they had done for six continuous hours in most intricate country. But just before they reached the pass a sad fatality occurred.

Lieutenant Wylie, of the 1st Battalion 2nd Ghoorkhas, had been exposing himself a good deal, and his commanding officer had enjoined him to be more careful. Very shortly afterwards, in compliance with the friendly suggestion just made him, he cautiously raised his head for a moment above a rock, when a stray bullet passed through his brain, killing him on the spot.

The enemy were very close at this time, and their fire was very hot, but Captain Macintyre, regardless of risk, went out and carried his comrade's body up to the pass.

All the orders for the retirement had been most carefully thought out by Brigadier-General Kempster, and the retirement had been arranged so that one regiment should relieve another in the arduous duty of protecting the rear. Further down the pass, in accordance with the orders issued before starting, were the 36th Sikhs under Lieutenant-Colonel Haughton, ready to cover the retirement of the 15th Sikhs.

The Zakka Khel Afridis had now induced the

Aka Khels to join them, and both tribes were actively engaging the 15th Sikhs on the pass, a large number of Zakka Khels attacking the Sikhs' left flank. As Colonel Abbott, commanding the latter, began to draw in the pickets from the adjoining hills preparatory to retiring, the enemy became very bold, and many losses occurred before he could assemble all his men in some sangars near the top of the hill. The total force under his command was now only about five companies, for many men were away on baggage duty or carrying the wounded.

The enemy, who were in increased numbers, now occupied a wood only about forty yards from the main sangar, and Colonel Abbott signalled to Brigadier-General Kempster, who was halted further back with the guns and main body, that the retirement was delayed by the presence of wounded men in the small sangar at the top of the hill. Captain Lewarne and his company had to wait here till the enemy's fire could be sufficiently controlled to enable the wounded men to be carried over a piece of ground in his immediate rear—a task of immense difficulty.

When Brigadier-General Kempster received Colonel Abbott's message, he at once sent orders for five companies of the 36th Sikhs and two companies of the Dorsets to return towards the 15th Sikhs and assist the retirement. Colonel Haughton, however, seeing the straits in which the 15th Sikhs were, had at once, anticipating these orders, started back with the company nearest him, and Captain Custance had also returned with another company 36th Sikhs. Major Des Vœux remained behind to bring on the other three companies of his regiment and the two companies of the Dorsets.

Captain Custance was the first to arrive to Colonel Abbott's assistance joining his forces with the four companies of the 15th Sikhs, the 5th under Captain Lewarne still holding the small sangar in front. As Captain Lewarne began to retire, the enemy, probably imagining the party was very much weaker than it really was, rushed out from the wood with a large number of swordsmen. Captain Lewarne very coolly halted and fronted the company, while Lieutenant Vivian promptly led up another company of the 15th Sikhs to his assistance, and together brought a withering fire to bear on the enemy, a fire before which the charging tribesmen actually seemed to melt away. The death of the twenty-one men of the 36th Sikhs at Saragarhi was thus amply avenged by their comrades of the 15th.

The losses on our side in the main sangar were unfortunately heavy: Colonel Abbott received a charge of slugs in the cheek; Captain Custance, who had just arrived with the first company of the 36th Sikhs, after receiving two bullets through the helmet was shot through the thigh, and both he and Colonel Abbott were being carried down the hill in stretchers when Colonel Haughton, with the next company of the 36th Sikhs, arrived on the scene. Major Des Vœux followed shortly afterwards with three more companies 36th Sikhs and half a company of Dorsets; the other one and a half companies of the Dorsets being left to hold some houses further down the road in order to give a point of *appui* for the troops on the pass to retire on.

Although Colonel Haughton had nominally ten companies of Sikhs and half a company of Dorsets under his command, so weakened were they from various causes that, when all the wounded had been sent on, scarcely more than two hundred men were left.

It was now getting dusk, and Colonel Haughton ordered a gradual retirement, and by the time the troops reached the bottom of the hill it was quite dark. A halt was made to re-form, and to search for a path above the nullah, for Colonel Haughton, with his great experience and knowledge of the Pathan, was unwilling to take his troops in the dark by the main path which followed the nullah bed.

At this moment, a heavy fire was suddenly opened on the troops from front, rear and flanks, and especially from some partly destroyed houses in front. Such a sudden attack might well have caused a commander less cool than Colonel Haughton to hesitate, but he, with perfect calmness and presence of mind, gave the order to fix bayonets and to advance against the houses, some 200 yards distant.

As soon as the order was given, the Dorset Regiment advanced with a cheer, and the Sikhs also shouting their war cry, swarmed up the slope, which was composed of a number of terraces, and dashed into the houses. The Pathans waited till their assailants were within ten paces before opening fire, and then every rifle and firearm they had blazed forth. Fortunately, owing to the darkness and to the fact that there was a high terrace just behind the houses, every shot but one was too high, and that dangerously wounded a Sikh native officer. A few of the tribesmen were shot when the houses were seized, and Lieutenant Munn, the Adjutant of the 36th Sikhs, ran one through with his sword.

The troops had at first occupied various buildings, but there being some danger of firing one into another in the dark, the "cease fire" was sounded, and the 15th Sikhs, the half company of the Dorsets, and three companies of the 36th Sikhs, all under Colonel Haughton, occupied one house. Major Des Vœux, with two companies 36th Sikhs, had seized another house, but finding it untenable, moved to a stronger one further away.

The house or group of houses which Colonel Haughton's troops had taken were still too hot from their recent burning to be occupied, so that the men had to be arranged in a semi-circle, with the main building behind them; and as no materials, such as stones, timber, or clods of earth were available, to make a barricade, the troops had to lie flat on the ground. Before all could get into position the enemy opened a heavy fire, killing Captain Lewarne, 15th Sikhs, and wounding Lieutenant Munn, 36th Sikhs, besides killing three Sepoys and wounding five others. Major Des Vœux's men fared better, for the house they had seized was sufficiently cool to enter, and materials were found round it of which a barricade could be made. The enemy kept up a desultory fire round both buildings till the moon began to rise, and then drew off.

Meanwhile it had fared very badly with the one and a half companies of the Dorset Regiment. Although nominally one and a half companies, there were only about thirty men in all, or two very small half companies, and with them were two officers who were attached to the Dorsetshire Regiment for duty, viz., Lieutenant Crooke, Suffolk Regiment, and Lieutenant Hales, East Yorkshire Regiment. Of these, Lieutenant Crooke was the senior, a very good officer, and who could be relied on not to lose his head; but both were quite unused to the country.

The house in which Major Des Vœux had left them could have been rendered very strong for defence, but it is believed that some men were heard moving on the road below the house, and when challenged, replied that they were Sikhs. Whether Lieutenant Crooke believed that the Sikhs were now retiring below him and that his party might join them, or whether he thought that the best chance of safety lay in trying to get back to camp, will probably never be known, for the accounts of the survivors were most conflicting.

In any case the party left the house, and one half company under Lieutenant Crooke appear to have gone by one path and the remaining half company by another. The latter half company were brought into camp intact by a sergeant, though Lieutenant Hales was killed, but it fared very badly with the other half company, who, bewildered by the darkness and intricacies of the nullah into which they had worked their way, got separated in some measure and were attacked by Pathans, for whom they were no match in the darkness.

Singly, or by twos and threes, they kept wandering into camp all night, but Lieutenants Crooke and Hales and twelve men failed to return, and were found the next morning in the nullah, where they had died facing fearful odds.

Private Vicary, who formed one of Lieutenant Crooke's party, and who had distinguished himself by bringing in a wounded man at Dargai from under a heavy fire, was one of the men who was wounded, but escaped. He was shot through the foot and then attacked by three Pathan swordsmen. The first he shot, the second he bayoneted, and the third he felled with his clubbed rifle, knocking the man's brains out. He then, wounded as he was, fell in with another wounded man, and brought him safely into camp.

There is no doubt as to the correctness of the above, for the medical officer in charge of the hospital where the two wounded men were quartered, saw Private Vicary's rifle, the butt of which bore marks of the Pathan's brains, and his boot had a hole drilled through it by a bullet, which had gone through the instep and out at the sole.

To return for a moment to the main body under Brigadier-General Kempster:—When the 36th Sikhs went back to the aid of the 15th Sikhs, the main body halted in the hope that they might be able to assist the retirement of the troops on the pass, but as darkness came on and neither artillery nor infantry could see to fire, the main body moved on to camp, and arrangements were made for a relief force to start next morning at daybreak.

Before it was light next morning, Colonel Haughton, whom no danger ever deterred, started out by himself under a heavy fire to reconnoitre and decide on the best method of removing the killed and wounded to camp without further loss. All the stretchers had been used up, but fortunately some native bedsteads were found in the houses, and on these the wounded were laid. The force then started off to cross some very intricate ground which lay between them and Major Des Vœux before it should get light enough to enable the enemy to find the range, the retirement being well covered by the half company of the Dorset Regiment under Lieutenant Cowie. As soon as the whole force was concentrated, the move was begun towards camp, and the relieving troops were shortly afterwards met with. The men, who had spent the night in the captured houses, suffered terribly from the cold, for the houses being without roofs afforded no shelter from the bitter frost, and the men had neither great-coats nor blankets.

The casualties were:

Dorsets. — Lieutenants Crooke and Hales (attached) and eleven men killed; eight men wounded.

1st Battalion 2nd Ghoorkhas. — Lieutenant Wylie and three men killed; five men wounded.

15th Sikhs.—Captain Lewarne and five men killed; Colonel Abbott and twenty-six men wounded.

36th Sikhs. — Four men killed; Captain Custance, Lieutenant Munn, and six men wounded.

No. 5. Bombay M.B.—One man wounded.

No. 8 M.B.R.A.—One man wounded.

Here again was a sad ending to what had otherwise been a most successful expedition. It was very difficult to ascertain exactly what was happening in the case of the defence of the pass and in the attack on the houses, so rapidly did events follow one another, and so impossible was it later on, owing to the darkness, for any officer to see more than what was proceeding in his immediate vicinity. As regards the fatality in the half company of the Dorset Regiment no one could give a clear account, but on one point all who were under Colonel Haughton's command on the night of the 16th November are unanimous, and that is that he, by extreme coolness and presence of mind, by a thorough grasp of the military situation, by quick decision, and by the confidence he inspired in every man under him, British or native, converted what, under a less capable leader, might have been a disaster, into a most brilliant feat of arms.

The enemy, who were confident of success, were completely surprised by the sudden and unimpeded charge on the houses; and though, most unfortunately, Colonel Haughton has since lost his life while gallantly leading his men in the action of the Shin Kamar Pass, his memory will survive not only among the 36th Sikhs, of whom he was such a model leader, but among all who had the privilege of seeing during the campaign how gallantly he fought and how skilfully he commanded.

CHAPTER XI.

MOVE TO BAGH—EXPEDITIONS TO DWATOI AND ESOR.

On the 18th November the first move, preparatory to shifting the whole camp to Bagh, was made by the 2nd Brigade and the divisional troops of the 1st Division under Major-General Symons. Bagh is about three-and-a-half miles distant from Camp Maidan, and is a place of notoriety in Tirah, as well as important from a military point of view. The Afridis regard it in some degree as sacred, and one of the few mosques which the irreligious tribesmen possess—a miserable hovel standing in a grove of trees—being situated here. The attack on the Khyber Pass and many other raids and expeditions were planned here, for it has always been the spot where great Afridi meetings have been held when any enterprise by the combined tribe was on foot.

From a military point of view it is of importance, because it is situated at the spot where the numerous tributaries of the Sher Darra finally combine to form the Sholaba, or twenty waters; and the Sholaba, flowing down a narrow and difficult valley or ravine, comes out at Dwatoi, the head of the Bara and Rajgul valleys.

There were many reasons why a move to Bagh was expedient after nearly three weeks' stay in Maidan Camp. Nearly all the forage and grain in the vicinity had been exhausted, and a move to Bagh threatened other sections of the Afridis, besides being desirable from a sanitary point of view, as camps, especially when animals have to be buried in considerable numbers, are apt to become foul and unhealthy.

On their arrival Major-General Symons's troops met with severe opposition, especially when the tribesmen found we had come to stay, for the place had merely been reconnoitred before. Captain Parker's battery, No. 2, Derajat, came under an especially severe fire, the enemy managing to creep up to within 500 yards of it. Captain Parker received a bullet through his clothes without its touching him, another grazed the ear of a subaltern, and a third carried away the hilt of another officer's sword.

Despite all this, the battery continued to make excellent practice, and the Queen's, the Yorkshire Regiment, and the 3rd Sikhs were at times hotly engaged. Second Lieutenant Edwards, of the Yorkshire Regiment, with a colour-sergeant and thirteen men, turned some tribesmen out of a house they were holding in an exceptionally brilliant manner, losing the colour-sergeant and one man; and many a junior officer led his men equally gallantly, for the enemy hung on to fortified towers and houses on many sides of the camp, and combined action against them was impossible. Small parties led by young officers turned the tribesmen out of one house after another in a way which won Major-General Symons's warm approbation, though the casualties, before all the enemy had been dislodged, were five men killed and twenty-two wounded.

No sooner had darkness set in than the tribesmen opened a hot fire on the camp; but all the troops not engaged in fighting had been entrenching its perimeter; and with pickets securely entrenched on surrounding hills, no further losses occurred, though bullets flew thick and fast.

On the 19th Sir William Lockhart and Staff, and the majority of the 2nd Division, advanced to Bagh, Brigadier-General Kempster with his brigade, strengthened by artillery and sappers and miners, remaining at Maidan Camp till the vast quantity of stores and supplies collected there had all been moved. Finally, on the 21st November, Camp Maidan was evacuated, and all the fortified towers and houses situated in it blown up or burnt.

The 15th Sikhs did not accompany the 3rd Brigade to Bagh on the 21st. This magnificent regiment had lost so heavily since the beginning of the campaign that Sir William Lockhart deemed it best, in the interests of the regiment itself, to give it a comparative rest on the line of communications. Before he left Maidan Camp he addressed the regiment on parade, and told them how worthily they had maintained, not only the credit of the regiment, but of the great Sikh Khalsa to which they belonged. Their place in the 3rd Brigade was afterwards taken by the 2nd Panjaub Infantry, who had hitherto been on the line of communications.

So constant was the firing into Camp Bagh

at night that it was finally determined to destroy a long line of fortified towers and houses, from whence the tribesmen emerged at dusk to annoy us in camp, for forbearance has its limits. On the 21st, as Brigadier-General Kempster's brigade was on the move between the two camps, Brigadier-General Gaselee's brigade moved out and set fire to all the fortified towers south of the camp on a front of about two miles.

I can only compare the smoke, as it rose and formed a dense pall over the whole country below, to a thick yellow fog such as London sees in November. The sun was quite unable to penetrate this pall, and for some three or four hours the absence of the accustomed sunshine gave one the feeling that a heavy fall of snow was imminent. A large number of towers nearer the camp had been destroyed on the previous day, and so salutary was the effect that after the 20th there was little, if any, night firing into Camp Bagh.

The Zakka Khels meanwhile continued their efforts to intercept convoys, but on the 20th were cleverly caught, for Major Kelly, R.E., hearing firing in the direction of the Arhanga Pass, hurried up No. 4 Company Madras Sappers, under Captain Wright, who were working not far off. This drove the tribesmen towards the head of the pass, and two companies of Gordon Highlanders hurried down one on each side of the ravine, caught the Zakka Khels between two fires, and accounted for some twenty or thirty of them.

As it was now the 21st of November, or three weeks since we had entered Afridi Tirah, and only four out of the eight Afridi tribes had sent in "jirgahs," Sir William Lockhart decided to announce the terms of the Government to the four already assembled, and this was accordingly done through Sir Richard Udny. He informed them that in Sayad Akbar's house at Warān, which we had destroyed on the 15th November, there had been found, among other letters, one from some Afridis in Kabul to the effect that the Turks had beaten our armies, that we had been turned out of Egypt, and could not send out troops by the Suez Canal, that India was ready to rise, and that altogether we were in great difficulties.

Sir Richard Udny pointed out the foolishness

of all this, and the smoke from the burning towers on every side helped to point the moral. As far as the Malikdin Khels, inhabiting the Sholaba Valley, and the Adam Khels were concerned, it had the desired effect, for the former, fortunately for us, made terms before we entered that terrible ravine in December.

On the 22nd a most adventurous, but highly successful, reconnaissance was made down the Sholaba defile to Dwatoi (or two waters), where the Rajgul and Shaloba streams combine and form the Bara river. Brigadier-General Westmacott commanded the force which Sir William Lockhart, Brigadier-General Nicholson, and a good many of the Staff accompanied. The troops were the Yorkshire Regiment (19th), the K.O.S.B's. (25th), the 36th Sikhs, the 1st Battalion 2nd and 3rd Ghoorkhas, the 28th Bombay Pioneers, No. 4 Bombay and No. 4 Madras Sappers and Miners, and two mountain batteries.

The 1st Battalion 2nd Ghoorkhas and the Yorkshire Regiment started before daybreak to crown the hills on either side of the ravine—the Ghoorkhas on the left, and the Yorkshires on the right. The

1st Battalion 3rd Ghoorkhas acted as advanced guard, and the 36th Sikhs as rearguard.

For the first two miles the valley is fairly open, and there was little or no opposition, so well did the troops on the flanks and the advanced guard do their work. After about two miles, however, the valley narrows until it becomes a gorge, with rocky and precipitous sides. So many subsidiary spurs are thrown out from the main range of hills on either side, that not only is the stream always winding in and out, flowing as it does between the teeth of two combs, so to speak, but it was absolutely impossible for the regiments on the main crests to search and clear all the cover afforded by these numerous spurs.

Quite apart, too, from the fact that the ravine was constantly commanded from spurs in front, which were thickly wooded in places, and afforded magnificent cover to sharp-shooters, it was also a most difficult matter, even without opposition, to make one's way along the ravine. To do so, the stream, knee-deep at times, had constantly to be forded and re-forded, and again in places the precipitous mountain-side had to be climbed, and a path made far up above the stream.

There was a semblance of a track occasionally, but so narrow and dangerous, that many a loaded transport animal lost its footing and fell crashing over the rocks into the rushing stream below; all along the stream, in the most difficult portion of the ravine, dead mules and ponies were lying when the column returned to Bagh.

The 1st Battalion 3rd Ghoorkhas were soon engaged in clearing and holding the spurs above the ravine, and sharp firing was going on all round. The 28th Bombay Pioneers took over the duties of advanced guard, and the K.O.S.B.'s. supported them, and so the column pushed on. Just before the ravine began to open out, some of the enemy's marksmen had found the exact range, and bullets were ploughing up the water at places where the stream had to be forded, and here, as the K.O.S.B.'s. moved up to reinforce the 28th Bombay Pioneers and help to clear off the enemy, four or five of their men were hit. Many of the marksmen also had the exact range of various points on the path along which it was necessary to pass, and Sir

William Lockhart's native orderly, on passing one of these points, was hit by no less than three bullets.

The most difficult portion of the ravine extends for about two miles, and then the valley begins to widen out; here the guns could again come into play, whereas in the ravine itself the close ranges from which the enemy's marksmen were firing, quite prohibited the use of artillery.

As the Pioneers pushed on in the direction of Dwatoi the enemy opened a heavy fire on them, resulting in four or five casualties, but the guns of No. 5 Bombay Mountain Battery greatly assisting, the Pioneers crossed the open space with a rush, and Dwatoi was seized.

It was about 5 P.M.; the men were wet to their waists; there was no food beyond what they carried in their haversacks. Many companies had to move out almost at once and picket the adjoining hills; and the troops had not even great-coats and blankets, whilst, to light a fire on picket was but to attract the enemy's bullets. Even Sir William Lockhart's baggage did not arrive, so the general, the officers, and the men were all equally without other food or warm clothing than what they had managed to carry with them; and, with the exception of a fortunate few who were able to find a house to go into, all the force spent a terribly cold night.

Great anxiety was felt for the transport, for had the enemy attacked it during its passage through the gorge heavy casualties must have resulted. Fortunately, all was well, and about 11 A.M. the next morning some of it began to appear, but it was not till 5 P.M. that the whole of it came in. Till that hour some of the troops were without food, except the little they had been able to bring with them when they started in the early morning of the day before.

Lieutenant-Colonel Haughton, who had been in command of the rearguard and was protecting the transport, saw that, owing to the terrible difficulties of the road, there was no chance of its being able to reach camp before nightfall. He therefore determined not to risk the loss of men, followers and animals by exposing them to a night attack when filing along the narrow path, and accordingly stopped all forward movement. The baggage was parked or formed up in a convenient spot, strong pickets were placed on the hills round the temporary camp, and so the night passed.

When it is considered that the total distance from Bagh to Dwatoi is under seven miles, and that the rearguard with the tail of the baggage which had started at 9 A.M. on the 22nd only reached camp at 5 P.M. on the 23rd, it shows better than I can possibly describe what the difficulties of the road were. The fact that there were seventeen degrees of frost at Dwatoi on the night of the 22nd, that all the troops had been wet to the waist, that many of them had empty stomachs, and that they had no fires to warm themselves by, or great-coats or blankets to lie in, will also convey a very clear idea of what they suffered that night.

During the 23rd the enemy seized a hill from which a picket had been withdrawn; but two companies of the K.O.S.B'.s under Colonel Dixon re-took the position in the most gallant way. The enemy, however, clung on so tenaciously to it that hand-to-hand fighting took place, the officers using their revolvers. The entrance into the Bara and the Rajgul valleys had now been reconnoitred, and the return to Bagh was fixed for the 24th.

The baggage was all loaded by daybreak and the force started off up the ravine again, the worst places on the road having been considerably improved the previous day by the Pioneers and Sappers. So expeditiously was the baggage got out of the camp and despatched on its way, that soon after 8 A.M. the rearguard under Colonel Haughton had moved off, and all the pickets had been withdrawn from the outlying hills.

The Afridis are not as a rule very early risers, and this expeditious movement had quite taken them by surprise; but they soon began their favourite tactics of harassing the rearguard.

The main crests on each side of the ravine were still being guarded by the Yorkshire Regiment and 1st Battalion 2nd Ghoorkhas, who had held them from the morning of the 22nd, and who of course at that height had experienced intense cold at night. The enemy, as I have said, made every effort to harass the rearguard; and so closely did they press and so straight did they shoot, that there were soon several casualties in the 36th Sikhs. To help carry some of the men who were not so severely wounded as to require the use of stretchers, some ambulance ponies were sent back. A few adventurous spirits among the Afridis tried to cut off these ponies, and dropped into the steep portion of the ravine without apparently being aware how strong a detachment of the 36th Sikhs was close behind.

Colonel Haughton was with the two rear companies of his regiment, and seeing that the enemy might now by an expeditious movement be caught between two fires, detached Captain Venour and a few men to try and cut these tribesmen off. This, Captain Venour completely succeeded in doing. The Afridis were caught in a trap, with precipitous walls of rock on two sides. On the other two sides were the 36th Sikhs, who all through the campaign had been awaiting the opportunity of avenging Saragarhi.

There was no escape for the tribesmen; the Sikhs met them hand-to-hand with the bayonet, Captain Venour being slightly wounded.

After this the Afridis contented themselves with shooting from long ranges; but so excellent were General Westmacott's dispositions, so well guarded were the flanks by the Ghoorkhas and the Yorkshire Regiment, and so admirably was the rearguard handled by Colonel Haughton, that the whole force, including baggage and rearguard, had reached Camp Bagh before dark.

It is now time to turn to the two regiments which had been doing such hard work on the flanks. The 1st Battalion 2nd Ghoorkhas, under Colonel Travers, had most difficult ground to move over on the left flank of the advance, and had one man killed and three men wounded early on the morning of the 22nd. The mountain crest they had to move along, while keeping parallel, or nearly so, to the advanced guard of the column below, was constantly broken by precipitous dips, so that the troops were frequently descending and again ascending steep mountain sides. They had a comparatively peaceful day on the 23rd, when the column was halted at Dwatoi, far below them, but had some brisk skirmishing on the return march of the 24th, and though there were many very narrow escapes, and butts and stocks of rifles were shot away, wonderful to relate, no casualties occurred.

The Yorkshire Regiment had done equally good work on the other side. So steep was the hill they had to climb, on leaving Camp Bagh, that no mules could accompany them; the mountain side had literally to be crawled up. As they were moving along the crest of the hill a few sharp-shooters were seen further down on a lower spur, and Lieutenant Jones, taking three men with him, boldly started off to try and turn the enemy out.

Not being able to discover their exact position, he determined to reconnoitre by himself—a very courageous but at the same time a very perilous undertaking. He was suddenly seen to jump on to a rock and empty his revolver, and then fall back. The three men hurried below to him, and Lieutenant Watson at once brought down another section of the company to his assistance; but when Lieutenant Jones was reached it was seen he was mortally wounded, and haste was made to put him into a stretcher. Lieutenant Watson divested himself of his coat to make a pillow for his comrade, but hardly had he done so than he was dangerously wounded, and a lance-corporal, who was helping him to place Lieutenant Jones on the stretcher, was shot dead.

Fortunately there were no more casualties in the Yorkshire, for both British and native regiments had taken a leaf out of their opponents' book, and become most skilful skirmishers. To do so, however, requires time, especially for troops brought up to take part in the campaign from districts of India where the nature of the country is entirely different; but sooner or later all the troops adapted themselves to the conditions which this guerilla warfare demanded.

As no mules had been able to accompany the Yorkshire Regiment on the 22nd, the great-coats, blankets, and supplies had to be conveyed up to them by hand on the 23rd, by which time they had been thirty-six hours without other food beyond what they carried with them at starting. So cold was it, too, in the nights and early mornings in this defile, that as the main column forded and reforded the river on their homeward march on the 23rd, the men's wet clothes began to freeze, and some of the ponies arrived in Camp Bagh with their manes and tails—which had been thoroughly wetted as they splashed through the river—still frozen hard.

The value of this reconnaissance was immense. It gave a very clear idea of the nature of the Bara and Rajgul valleys, and the experience gained in traversing the Sholaba defile was of great value when the time came for the whole Second Division to pass that way.

The casualties from the 22nd to the 24th in this reconnaissance were:—

Yorkshire Regiment.—One officer and one man killed; one officer wounded.

K.O.S.B.'s.—One man killed; six men wounded.

No. 5 Bombay Mountain Battery.—One man wounded.

1st Battalion 2nd Ghoorkhas.— Three men wounded.

1st Battalion 3rd Ghoorkhas.—One man killed; three men wounded.

28th Bombay Pioneers.—One man killed; five men wounded.

36th Sikhs.—Two men killed; one officer and fifteen men wounded.

On the 24th orders were issued for the whole of

R

the heavy baggage, and also a large proportion of the Headquarter Staff, to return to Shinawari, the idea being that the First Division from the Mastura valley, and the Second Division from Camp Bagh, should move down, with the minimum of transport and baggage animals, to a camp on the Bara river and join hands with the column under Brigadier-General Hammond.

To this end, also, the sick and wounded, and all men who were in a weakly state of health, were sent back to Shinawari, and the hospitals reduced their establishment of stores, tents, and followers as far as possible.

The Headquarters and Half Battalion of the Royal Scots Fusiliers arrived from Kohat on the 25th, and were attached to the Second Division; and on the 26th a force under Brigadier-General Gaselee, composed of the Queen's (2nd), the 3rd Sikhs, 2nd Battalion 4th Ghoorkhas, 28th Bombay Pioneers, No. 1 Kohat and No. 5 Bombay Mountain Batteries, started in the direction of the Lozaka Pass west of Camp Bagh, which leads into the Chamkanni and Massuzai country.

On the 27th Sir William Lockhart, Brigadier-

General Nicholson, and others of the Staff, taking with them the Yorkshire Regiment (19th), Half Battalion Royal Scots Fusiliers (21st), the 1st Battalion 2nd Ghoorkhas, and No. 2 Derajat Mountain Battery, started to catch up Brigadier-General Gaselee. The 28th Bombay Pioneers, who had merely gone to improve the road, returned to Camp Bagh on the evening of the 26th.

The reasons for making this expedition were numerous. In the first place both the Chamkannis and Massuzais (Orakzai tribes) had been very troublesome, and had constantly fired into Colonel Hill's camp at Sadda in the Kurram; and they, especially the Chamkannis, were concerned in the attack on the picket of the Kapurthala Imperial Service Infantry attached to Colonel Hill's force, when a native officer and thirty-five men had been cut up. Another reason was, that in his proclamation to the tribes, Sir William Lockhart had announced his intention of visiting the whole country; and by moving over the Lozaka Pass entirely fresh ground would be explored, and touch gained with Colonel Hill's column.

On the 26th Brigadier-General Gaselee advanced

towards the foot of the Lozaka Pass and encountered some opposition. A company of the Queen's, under Lieutenant Engledue, who were posted on the left flank to guard the advance, saw some sangars, and not knowing if they were occupied or not, advanced to seize them, creeping up from behind. The enemy who were holding them, and whose attention must have been turned in some other direction, were completely surprised. Six were bayoneted, and six more were shot, one man only of the Queen's being killed; the other casualties that day being one man Yorkshire Regiment and three Ghoorkhas killed, with five Ghoorkhas wounded. The next day the Ghoorkha Scouts and 3rd Sikhs were pushed forward to seize a long, well-wooded spur jutting out from the main ridge, and which lies south of the Kahn Darra Pass.

This latter appeared an easier one than the Lozaka, and accordingly the attack was directed against it. The pass was seized with but slight opposition, but it was found an impossibility to get the baggage over it that day; so Colonel Collins, commanding the Queen's, with half his regiment, a battery, and a company of Sappers and Miners, were sent into the Massuzai Valley. Brigadier-General Gaselee, with the 3rd Sikhs and the 2nd Battalion 4th Ghoorkhas, remained on the pass, and the baggage and transport with the remaining troops encamped at the foot of it.

All the troops who were separated from their baggage had a very trying night without food or blankets, but luckily wood was plentiful, and large fires were lit. An attack was made on the baggage during the night, and repulsed with loss to the enemy, the casualties on the 27th being one man 3rd Sikhs and two mule drivers killed.

Hearing from Brigadier-General Gaselee of the difficult nature of the pass, and that the baggage had not crossed, Sir William Lockhart and the troops with him encamped further back, and did not advance. The enemy also harassed the march of these troops a good deal, though they had been told that if our advance was unmolested their towers and fortified houses would be spared. As they had not chosen to listen, all the buildings from which our troops were fired at were burnt to the ground; our casualties being one man Royal Scots killed and two wounded, and one man Yorkshire Regiment killed.

Early next morning—the 28th—Brigadier-General Gaselee set the men to work at improving the road over the pass. The road down on the other side was much easier than it was up, and most of the troops pressed forward to join the force under Colonel Collins, who had gone on some four miles towards a village called Dargai, or Dargai Towi—not to be confounded with the Dargai, the scene of the two fights. It was impossible to push the baggage up so far, and only a portion reached Dargai, the rest of it remaining on the pass with a strong guard. The troops again passed a night in the cold; but these things are unavoidable when a force is moving in a roadless country with pack transport, and that not all of first-rate quality.

The scenery of the Massuzai country is magnificent and far more beautiful than the Maidan Valley. The hills are densely wooded, the valleys well-watered, the soil fertile, the houses strongly built, and everything points to the inhabitants being wealthy and skilful agriculturists.

On the 29th, the main column pushed on to Dargai village, and here the inhabitants (Massuzais) came forward to tender their submission ; but the rearguard bringing in the baggage were meanwhile engaged in very close fighting with the Kambar Khels, who had followed up and over the pass. The rearguard consisted of two companies Yorkshire Regiment and three of the Royal Scots Fusiliers, with No. 2 Derajat Mountain Battery, and was most admirably handled by Colonel Spurgin. They kept the enemy at bay, and the whole of the troops and baggage got into camp by about midnight on the 29th with seventeen casualties.

On the 30th the main column resumed the march to Esor, where a junction was effected with Colonel Hill's column from Sadda. Some of the troops remained temporarily at Dargai under Colonel Spurgin to enforce the submission of the Massuzais who appeared to have rather changed their minds as to submitting when they found their rifles were wanted ; and stoutly denied having any. No sooner, however, had one tower in the village been set alight than the rifles demanded were immediately produced. Another tribe, the Mamozai

Orakzais, were also quite ready to submit and pay the fine demanded, but the Chamkannis continued recalcitrant.

A column under Colonel Hill was despatched on the 1st December to march to Thati, the capital, so to speak, of the Chamkannis. The force consisted of the 2nd Battalion 4th Ghoorkhas, one wing 1st Battalion 5th Ghoorkhas, the 12th Bengal Infantry, the Kapurthala Infantry (Imperial Service Troops), three hundred dismounted men of the 6th Bengal Cavalry and Central India Horse, No. 4 Company Bombay Sappers, No. 1 Kohat Mountain Battery, and the Ghoorkha Scouts.

Colonel Hill divided his troops into two columns; but owing to the fact that the country was quite unknown and that the enemy made a strong resistance, co-operation was not effected in time. The column under Colonel Hill, moving by a mountain path, reached the vicinity of the Chamkanni Valley in very good time. The other column under Colonel Gordon, moving by the river gorge, was greatly delayed by the difficult ground, and as it would have been too late to destroy the village towers when a junction between the two columns had been effected, the troops began to return to Camp Esor.

The enemy pressed very heavily on the retirement, and Lieutenant Battye, 6th Bengal Cavalry, was killed, Lieutenant Villiers Stewart, 5th Ghoorkhas, dangerously wounded, and Lieutenant Pennington, 12th Bengal Cavalry, slightly so, with six men killed, and sixteen wounded.

Sir William Lockhart had purposed moving on the 2nd of December, but as the Chamkannis had to be punished, he deferred his departure for a day, and despatched Colonel Hill against Thati with a force consisting of half a battalion of the Queen's, the 3rd Sikhs, the 4th and 5th Ghoorkhas, the Ghoorkha Scouts, and the Kohat Mountain Battery. The Ghoorkha Scouts under Lieutenant Lucas did most of the fighting; they swarmed up a precipitous hill, and as soon as the 5th Ghoorkhas appeared, they left some forty men to cover the advance of the remaining forty, and dashed at some sangars, the enemy in which had their attention considerably distracted by the near appearance of the 5th Ghoorkhas.

When the tribesmen saw the forty little Ghoorkhas

led by Lieutenant Lucas advancing on them with the bayonet they fired a volley, and with drawn swords stood up to receive the charge. The covering party of the Scouts, however, put a volley into them the moment they stood up in the sangars, and the sight of the forty or fifty Ghoorkhas, with bayonets fixed and simply shouting with delight at the prospect of a hand-to-hand fight, disconcerted the Chamkanni warriors, and though they waited till the charge had got to within twenty yards, they could stand no longer, and all organized resistance was over for the day.

All the towers in the valley were burned, some fifty villages, including Thati, losing their defences; and when the force withdrew the Chamkannis had no further heart for the fight. The casualties were Major Vansittart, 5th Ghoorkhas, slightly wounded, and two men killed and three wounded. The failure of the operations on the 1st had been amply atoned for by the brilliant success of those of the 2nd.

On the 3rd, Colonel Hill's force moved back to Sadda, and Sir William Lockhart returned to Camp Bagh, where he arrived on the 6th December, marching *via* Pshotandai, Khanki Bazar, and the Chingakh Pass, neither his column nor Colonel Hill's meeting with any further opposition.

The remaining Orakzai tribes had in the meanwhile practically complied with the terms in full, and all was quiet in the Mastura Valley. Of the Afridis, the Adam Khels and the Malikdin Khels (who occupy the most difficult portion of the Sholaba defile) had tendered their submission. The Kuki Khels, occupying the Rajgul Valley, had promised to hand in the rifles demanded from them by the time we arrived at Dwatoi. Sir William Lockhart sent a notice to the tribes who had not submitted, to say that he was only leaving Tirah to avoid the cold; but in case of non-compliance with the terms would return in the spring, and would meanwhile attack them in their winter quarters.

In the next chapter I shall endeavour to show how obdurate the other tribes, more especially the Zakka Khels, remained, notwithstanding the threat of a spring campaign.

CHAPTER XII.

THE MARCH DOWN THE BARA AND MASTURA VALLEYS.

When Sir William Lockhart left Camp Bagh on the 27th November to join hands with Colonel Hill's column at Esor, the preparations for the move of the 2nd Division to Barkai or Swaikot, on the Bara river near Peshawur, proceeded busily. All heavy baggage and surplus stores were packed up and sent off to Mastura, advantage being taken at the same time to utilise along the lines of communication such animals as, though fit for light work, might break down on the difficult march from Camps Bagh and Mastura to Swaikot; the latter being the point on the Bara river where the junction with Brigadier-General Hammond's column was to be effected.

All these surplus stores, together with those of the 1st Division at Mastura, were then passed back along the line of communications to Khusalgarh, and thence by rail to Peshawur. The

A GORGE ON THE ROAD BETWEEN FORT LOCKHART AND KARAPPA.

[*To face page* 252.

transport animals which had conveyed them were marched from Kohat to Peshawur, through the Kohat Pass, ready to convey the stores from thence to the various camps where the main column might be located. Preparations also were made so that both 1st and 2nd Divisions should be supplied with food sufficient to ration them up till the 14th December, the idea being that the base should now be changed from Kohat to Peshawur (the old line of communications however being temporarily maintained as far as Shinawari), and that the main column when it joined Brigadier-General Hammond's force should be supplied from Peshawur direct.

On the 3rd December the Field Post Offices which, under the able superintendence of Mr. Van Someren and his energetic assistants, had been supplying us daily with letters and papers in a way which reflects the greatest possible credit on all concerned, began to move off to Peshawur *viâ* Khusalgarh to be in readiness at the new camp when we arrived. From the 3rd to the 14th December, therefore, we were left without news of the outside world, as the telegraph department also closed, taking up as it went its wire, which had been so persistently cut and as regularly mended.

I have hitherto omitted all mention of the native shopkeepers. A large number of these men, braving the risks of the road, had made their very welcome appearance at Camp Maidan about the 10th of November. It was some time before even the Commissariat Department had been able to get any but the most necessary supplies up to Camp Maidan from Karappa, and regiments had to temporarily leave their field bakeries behind them when we moved from there. The consequence was that for the first ten days at Camp Maidan our staple diet was tinned Australian beef and Commissariat biscuits; bread, potatoes, milk, butter, eggs or vegetables were unprocurable—still more so whiskey; and even fresh meat was at first somewhat difficult to get.

The arrival of the bakeries, of the Commissariat stores, and of native dealers, changed all this. The latter brought with them whiskey, jams, tinned milk and butter, cheese, etc., and even eggs, but of a doubtful freshness; and though the prices were very high one could not call them exorbitant, considering the risks these merchants ran both in regard to life and property. It is only when one has been very short of the kinds of food which one has almost got to look on as necessaries rather than luxuries, that one appreciates the change from biscuits, tinned beef and Commissariat rum to the more ordinary sorts of meat and drink.

As the post office, telegraph office, tents, and heavy baggage left Camp Bagh, and day after day some officers of the Headquarter or Divisional Staff took their departure for Peshawur, the camp began to wear a most desolate appearance. About the 3rd of December most ominous signs of snow or rain began to appear, and as the thermometer was registering twenty degrees of frost at night, doubts were expressed as to whether we should be clear of Maidan before the snow came on us. Major-General Symons with the Divisional Staff of the 2nd Division had left Camp Bagh about the 28th November, to join the 1st Brigade (Brigadier-General Hart's) at Mastura; the latter having, in the meanwhile, thoroughly reconnoitred the Mastura Valley within reach of the camp.

The Transport officers had been busily engaged in weeding out all the indifferent animals; the useless ones being shot. Those which were weak, but still fit for light work, were utilised, as I have described above, in carrying the spare stores to Kohat and Khusalgarh, and about three thousand fresh animals of good stamina were brought up to Tirah and distributed among the regiments of the two divisions, so that all was ready for a start as soon as Sir William Lockhart returned.

The route taken by him during his reconnaissance to Esor is approximately shown by a thin red line on the map. After leaving Khanki Bazar, he crossed into Maidan by a pass called the Chingakh, about five miles west of the Arhanga Pass, and over 8,000 feet high, arriving at Bagh on the 6th. A column had moved out from Karappa up the Khanki Valley to meet him, bringing up supplies, and principally composed of the 2nd and 30th Punjaub Infantry. The 2nd Punjaub Infantry now joined Sir William Lockhart's force, and marching to Bagh took the place of the 15th Sikhs in the 3rd Brigade, while the 30th Punjaub Infantry returned to Karappa with the sick and wounded, and then proceeded to Mastura to join the 1st Brigade. Brigadier-General Hammond's column had meanwhile been busily engaged in improving the road from Bara, *viâ* Ilam Gudr, to Swaikot, close to Barkai, where it arrived on the 7th December.

On this date began the march of the 2nd Division from Bagh to Dwatoi by the difficult Sholaba defile. The 4th Brigade (Brigadier-General Westmacott's), with Major-General Yeatman-Biggs, and the Divisional Staff 2nd Division, and accompanied by Sir William Lockhart, moved off very early, leaving the 3rd and 2nd Brigades at Bagh, the former to follow next day, whilst the 2nd (Brigadier-General Gaselee's) moved off to Mastura to join the 1st Division. The advanced guard and flanking parties of the 4th Brigade were formed by the 3rd Ghoorkhas, the 28th Bombay Pioneers, a wing 2nd Punjaub Infantry, and No. 4 Company Madras Sappers and Miners, and while the Pioneers and the Sappers worked at the road (the beginning of which had been considerably improved by the 2nd Division Sappers under Major Kelly, R.E., some days previously), the 3rd Ghoorkhas and 2nd

S

Punjaub Infantry crowned and held the heights on each side.

The Malikdin Khels, who inhabit the most difficult and dangerous portion of the ravine, had already paid in a considerable portion of their fine, and had been told that if they did not molest the march of the column their towers and houses would be spared. It was well for them, and certainly for us, that they remained quiet, for while we could have done immense damage to them by burning their towers and fortified houses, they might, notwithstanding all our military precautions (none of which were neglected), have greatly harassed our march through the defile and inflicted on us heavy loss.

The head of the troops reached Dwatoi about 11 A.M., brushing away some slight opposition, and when the K.O.S.B.'s proceeded in the evening to picket some adjoining hills they were heavily fired on up to a late hour at night.

The 3rd Ghoorkhas, commanded by Colonel Pulley, did splendid work all that day; some of them, after guarding the crests of the hills, which involved most arduous marching, had to go on picket duty at night, and were again called for on the 8th, so that they had continuous work for thirty-six hours. It was a fine moonlight night on the 7th, and as there had been no opposition during the day the baggage was able to push on, the bulk of it reaching camp early on the morning of the 8th. The total number of animals with this column did not much exceed 7,000, and yet, with no opposition, with a road considerably improved, and with really good animals, the baggage took from 7 P.M. to 3 A.M. in covering six and a half miles, so difficult was the mountain defile. The 3rd Brigade Commissariat stores had accompanied the 4th Brigade baggage, and so great was the block ahead that this transport was only able to advance about four miles on the 7th, and thus greatly retarded the advance of the 3rd Brigade on the 8th.

On this day the 3rd Brigade started about 7 A.M. in drizzling rain, which looked every moment as if it would turn to snow. As they moved off to Dwatoi, and the 2nd Brigade to Mastura, men, women and children of the Malikdin and Adam Khel tribes rushed into the camp in the hopes of picking up grain, etc., left behind, so famine-stricken were they by their long sojourn in the mountains above Maidan. These two tribes, especially the old men, women and children, must have felt thankful that their jirgahs had made terms, and that the majority of their houses remained intact.

Owing to the Brigade Commissariat still blocking the road, the head of the 3rd Brigade could only march four miles, and had to camp for the night, while the rear of the column, which was marching, or rather standing about in the hopes of getting on, only accomplished three miles between 7 A.M. and 10 P.M. All the troops and the baggage eventually reached Camp Dwatoi by 5 P.M. on the 9th. The slow progress on the 8th, and the consequent waiting about which it entailed, was a most trying experience; the rain fell most of the time; the river, which had constantly to be forded, was icy cold, and two native soldiers, who were only slightly sick the day before, died in the dhoolies in which they were being carried.

To return for a moment to the 4th Brigade at Dwatoi. On the 8th the Kuki Khels, who, instead of handing in their rifles as they had promised, had, on the contrary, opposed our advanced guard when it reached Dwatoi, were holding a hill which commands the entrance to the Rajgul Valley, and kept firing on our pickets from there. Two companies, one of the 36th Sikhs, commanded by Lieutenant Van Someren, and one of the 3rd Ghoorkhas, under Lieutenant West, who lost his life a few days later, climbed up this hill in the most gallant style. Covered by the fire of some mountain guns, and skilfully led, they dislodged the enemy with a loss to themselves of only one man killed and four wounded. The Ghoorkhas engaged were men who had been marching and fighting for thirty-six hours on end, and yet they dashed up the hill like boys just released from school.

On the 9th the punishment of the Kuki Khels began. A column under Brigadier-General Westmacott, and which Sir William Lockhart accompanied, marched up the Rajgul Valley and completely destroyed all the towers and defences. The valley is an extremely difficult one, being in places only a defile, and inexperienced troops under a less capable leader might have suffered heavy losses; but these troops, keeping the enemy at a distance, and with the batteries making excellent practice, made havoc of the Kuki Khel stronghold, inflicted considerable loss on the enemy, and returned to camp with only four casualties.

On the 10th began the march down the Bara Valley; and it was persistently harassed from beginning to end by the enemy, who consisted principally of Zakka Khels, though possibly many other tribesmen joined in. In fact, from the morning of the 10th till the evening of the 14th some part of the troops were almost continually under fire.

The country was quite unknown to us, but it was thought we should reach the Bara river camp and join Brigadier-General Hammond's column in about four marches. The morning of the 10th was bitterly cold; a piercing wind was blowing down the valley; and hard times were evidently in store, especially for the shivering native followers, who, in common with all the troops, would have to constantly wade through the icy Bara stream.

The 4th Brigade (Brigadier-General Westmacott's) led the advance; then came the baggage hospitals, etc., of both brigades, a total of about 12,000 animals; and the 3rd Brigade brought up the rear.

It had been arranged that the 4th Brigade, with which Sir William Lockhart marched, should proceed to a place called Sandana, or thereabouts, some seven miles ahead; while the 3rd Brigade marched to a camp at or near Karana, about four miles distant. The Bara Valley was wide at its upper end and the going was easy, for there were many dry rice beds; and though the stream flowed sometimes on one side of the valley and sometimes on the other, occasionally breaking up into several channels, there was nothing to prevent the transport moving on a wide front by several paths and fording the stream at various places.

The transport drivers, as a rule slow and apathetic, seemed, once we started, to have brightened up at the thought of the nearness of British territory. The animals, like the drivers, felt the cold severely, and stepped out briskly; and the baggage moved along in a broad front, at a very different pace to that which it had been obliged to move in single file along a narrow mountain path. We were not able to congratulate ourselves for long, however, for as the last of the rearguard began to leave Camp Dwatoi and the pickets were withdrawn from the hills, the enemy came swarming round; and one of the Royal Scots Fusiliers was shot dead in the ranks as his company were falling in. There was, moreover, a good deal of firing, from the high hills on each side, into the flanks of the 4th Brigade and of the transport.

Hardly had night set in after reaching our camp when a very cold drizzling rain began to fall, and every one who had not got a waterproof sheet to form a *tente d'abri* or a native house to sleep in was completely wet through. The pickets round the camps were continually fired on during the night; and the casualties in the 3rd Brigade were six, and in the 4th Brigade seven, including Lieutenant Fowke, Dorset Regiment, severely wounded.

It had been intended that the 3rd Brigade should start early next morning and catch up the 4th Brigade; but this, as it turned out, was impossible. The rain, though it had been threatening for days in Maidan, does not as a rule fall before Christmas at a much lower altitude, so it came rather as a surprise.

The 3rd Brigade, which left Camp Dwatoi late in the morning to allow the 4th Brigade and all the baggage to get well ahead, only reached its camp late in the afternoon. For tactical reasons, a camping ground had been selected which was some way up above the river bed, and was approached by steep paths. After the rain of the previous night, which continued without intermission on the 11th, these paths became so slippery that it was impossible for laden animals to move on them, and a long *détour* in single file had to be made by the baggage in order to regain the river bed.

The Pioneer regiment and both companies of Sappers and Miners were ahead with the 4th Brigade, consequently little, if anything, could be done to improve the roads out of camp. Added to this the men, and more especially the followers, were wet through and chilled to the bone; the bedding and hospital tents were heavy with rain; the whole camp was deep in mud, and day broke quite an hour later than usual. Small wonder is it then that the 3rd Brigade were not ready to start as soon as intended. It was 11 A.M. before all the baggage was down off the hill, for animals kept constantly falling, and the drivers were too benumbed with cold to give much help in taking off and readjusting the loads, the whole of which work fell on the troops.

The 4th Brigade had, meanwhile, started on its march to Sher Khel, some ten miles distant from its camping ground, and some thirteen miles distant from that of the 3rd Brigade (Brigadier-General Kempster's); this latter having to throw out troops to guard its flanks, which would otherwise have been protected in a great measure by the flanking troops of the 4th Brigade.

No sooner had the transport gained the river bed and the rearguard commenced to leave the camp, than the enemy began to press from all sides, and bullets kept constantly whizzing overhead, a thud now and again showing that a bullet had found its billet. Nearly all the firing was from Lee-Metford rifles, and one could count shot after shot in quick succession, followed by a pause; then, rapid firing would again recommence, a sure sign that the tribesmen were using magazines. In the marches in Tirah the trouble had been to get the transport and their drivers along; now, the difficulty was to keep them back.

Benumbed with cold, with their feet bruised by knocking against the boulders when constantly fording the stream, the drivers pressed on. Terrified by the bullets which kept flying over their heads and occasionally knocking over a man or a mule, they tugged at the reins of the leading animal, quite regardless of how the loads were riding, or whether the last two animals of the three in their charge were coming on behind.

Frequently one of the animals in rear would break its chain or slip its bridle, and get detached from the mule in front; but the driver, unconscious of anything except the cold and misery he was suffering, and dreading each moment that a bullet would hit him, kept blindly on, till in some cases only main force would stop him. It may be thought I am exaggerating; but, so far from doing so, I am unable to find words to express the sort of panic, combined with stupor, which possessed the followers that day. The troops on baggage duty, British and native, had double work thrown on them, because most drivers were unable from cold and fear to even keep the animals still while loads were being readjusted.

If any one who reads this still remains incredulous, I would ask him to look at Zola's "Débâcle," or, better still, Von Hoenig's "Twenty-four Hours of Moltke's Strategy," and then see how brave soldiers, both in the French and German armies, were at times seized with panic. At Gravelotte, where Steinmetz's force was repeatedly hurled back in its assaults on the French left, panic after panic took place among some of the German troops, so much so that they fell back to the rear and walked straight on through their own guns, like men distraught; nothing could stop them.

If these things can happen to disciplined troops — and history is full of such instances — what wonder is it if poor, miserable native followers — a large number of them from the Madras Presidency, and therefore absolutely unaccustomed to such cold — should, for once in a way, have lost their heads and been deaf to all remonstrances and orders? It was the same thing with the dhooly bearers, the men whose duty it is to carry the sick and wounded in litters. They seemed barely able to carry even the empty litters through the rushing stream. As the wounded accumulated, the soldiers, British or native, had to assist in carrying their comrades; in some cases without any help at all from the dhooly bearers.

In this way the 3rd Brigade pushed on. Frequent halts were made to enable any transport in the rear to close up with the remainder, and to send fresh troops out to the flanks. The heavy rain, which kept on without intermission, had made the rice fields, etc., which would have been quite easy-going the previous day, into quagmires. Notwithstanding this, the mule-drivers constantly endeavoured to take short cuts over them, and thus avoid moving in the stony river-bed and crossing the icy-cold stream. Staff officers, transport officers, and the men with the baggage made every effort to keep the drivers to the river-bed; but, to do so, twenty times the number of transport officers would have been necessary, for a mule-driver, seeing what he thought was a short cut across some fields, would make a dash for it.

The ground appeared fairly firm at first, and ten, twenty, or thirty more drivers would follow the first one. Before they could be stopped and turned back, the leading driver would, perhaps, have reached a deep ditch or dyke. He would then attempt to pull the leading animal across it. The first mule would suddenly jump it, the second and third holding back, and one out of the three would fall into the ditch with the load beneath him. If, as happened in some cases, the leading animal got over, and the attachment between the first and second animals broke, the driver held on his way regardless. It was not that they deliberately left the other animals behind, but cold and fear had bereft them of their senses.

When the column halted in a narrow portion of the valley the transport had perforce to halt behind it, but the moment the column moved, the transport swept on like a pent-up stream suddenly released, sometimes on a front of one hundred yards, and sometimes on a front of half a mile. Each driver occasionally made for what he thought would be a short cut, and if not turned back in time probably got his animals bogged in crossing a road, or became hopelessly entangled in some deep dyke. All that the followers appeared to think of was to reach somehow or other the comparative safety of the next camp, and to have a fire to warm themselves by; all other considerations were as nothing.

About 5 P.M. the head of the 3rd Brigade column arrived in sight of the 4th Brigade camp, and it lay with Brigadier-General Kempster to decide as to whether to press on or to camp at a village close by.

On the 8th, 9th, and 10th the 3rd Brigade had been on rearguard duty, and though no fighting had occurred on the first two days, such work is always harassing. On the 10th and 11th the rearguard had continuous fighting. If the whole division became united, not only would the 4th Brigade take the rearguard duty, but the protection of the camp containing both brigades would fall less heavily on the 3rd Brigade than if they were to camp apart.

The road to the 4th Brigade camp seemed easy; the transport was reported to be well up, and

Brigadier-General Kempster, after some consideration, decided to press on.

The troops of the advanced guard and of the main column arrived in the 4th Brigade camp at Sher Khel before dusk, but darkness came on rapidly, and the rain continued without intermission. The sight of the camp fires made the mule drivers more anxious than ever to get on, and many of them, leaving the river-bed, made a bee-line for the lights ahead.

Now began the chief disaster of the march, for animals got bogged in all directions, or slipped up in watercourses and could not get out. The drivers in many cases left them and went into houses to get firewood; dhooly bearers put down their dhoolies and did likewise; others broached, or found a cask of rum already broached, and got so hopelessly drunk that three of them who came into camp died from the effects during the night. The rearguard and the tail of the baggage was not so near as the officer commanding the 3rd Brigade had believed it to be; for the driving rain and mist made it very difficult to see. As the rearguard, under Major Downman (Gordon Highlanders), followed up, they found, about three miles from camp, a large number of animals whose loads were off, entangled in ditches and watercourses, and whose drivers were benumbed with cold.

The enemy meanwhile were firing from all sides, and Major Downman took the extremely wise step of seizing some houses near and entrenching himself for the night. The troops with him were one company Gordon Highlanders, half company Dorset Regiment, half company 2nd Punjaub Infantry, and about three companies 1st Battalion 2nd Ghoorkhas; these were heavily encumbered with wounded.

As soon as the Afridis divined Major Downman's intention of seizing the houses, they attempted to forestall him, but Captain Uniacke, with some Gordon Highlanders, made a dash for the buildings and captured them. Once the troops were inside, the enemy was easily repulsed. It fared very badly meanwhile with the baggage animals and drivers who were just behind the main column when it reached the camp.

Between 7 and 8 P.M. heavy firing was heard outside the camp; for the enemy had now come in between the rearguard and the main column, and attacked the rear of the baggage and a party escorting some wounded men. These men were being carried by their comrades, the dhooly-bearers having by this time either disappeared in the darkness or become physically incapable of carrying any weight at all, when a sudden attack was made on the small party. Some of the men were so exhausted by the weight of the litters or dhoolies, that Surgeon-Major Beevor was himself helping to carry one of the wounded when this happened. Fortunately the darkness prevented the enemy from taking good aim, though they were only twenty yards off, and the gallant medical officer and the men with him repulsed their assailants, stuck to the wounded, and brought them into camp without further mishaps.

Early on the morning of the 12th, Brigadier-General Kempster with two battalions and a battery went out to assist in bringing in Major Downman's force, which was beleaguered by the enemy in the houses where they had spent the night; another half battalion went out to try and bring in the stray followers and animals and pick up some of the numerous loads which had been dropped. A good deal of the baggage and a number of animals were recovered; but few of the followers who had not found their way to camp escaped. Some had been shot or cut down, or had been stripped of their clothes and died of the cold, while others again had succumbed to the effects of the rum they had drunk in such large quantities the night before.

The enemy had made continual attacks on Major Downman's troops at daybreak, and had killed one man of the Gordons and wounded three more by a single volley. All the troops were safely in camp by 11 A.M., but there had been heavy casualties in addition to those amongst the followers. Captain Norie, 1st Battalion 2nd Ghoorkhas, had his arm shattered by a bullet; Lieutenant Williams, Hampshire Regiment, a transport officer, had a bullet through his leg, and there were some forty men killed and wounded—amongst whom the Gordon Highlanders had four men killed and eleven wounded—and the 1st Battalion 2nd Ghoorkhas two killed and nine wounded. Many followers and a large number of transport animals were killed and missing.

As it turned out, the losses would probably have

been less had the 3rd Brigade not pushed on so far on the 11th, but it was impossible to foresee that the baggage would at the last moment go so hopelessly astray and get entangled in the water-courses, which were close up to the camp. It was pure ill-luck that this should have happened, and it must in a very large measure be attributed to the rain, which considerably curtailed the two hours of daylight and hid the enemy's movements.

It was absolutely necessary for the force to halt for a day on the 12th. Not only had the rearguard under Major Downman (which though skilfully handled had lost heavily) to be extricated from the buildings they were holding, but the wounded required the medical attention which it had been impossible to give them.

Some of them had undergone extreme agony, and Captain Norie, 1st Battalion 2nd Ghoorkhas, whose arm had been shattered the day before, and who had borne his terrible sufferings with wonderful fortitude, had to have it amputated at the shoulder as soon as he was carried into camp; many other operations also had to be performed, so that the medical officers were busy all the day. The animals, too, greatly required a day's rest, for it is impossible, as a rule, to feed them on the march except with grain, as there is no time to forage at the end of the day.

The rain, which had poured down for more than twenty-four hours, stopped during the night of the 11th, and the sunshine, never more welcome or more needed, shone out again the next morning. This enabled the clothes, bedding, and hospital tents which had been wetted through by the continuous rain to be spread out and dried; and what was more, it put renewed sense and vitality into the native followers, who in extreme cold become mentally as well as physically benumbed, and seem incapable of understanding, much less obeying any order.

As the mist cleared away and the sun shone out, all the hills round were seen to be covered with snow, down to within a few hundred feet above the level of the camp, clearly showing we had not left Maidan a day too soon, and accounting for the very great cold we had experienced the previous day.

Advantage was taken of our halt to make several roads from the camp down to the river valley, and to send out parties to the neighbouring houses for forage and wood. All these were fired on, and from about 3 P.M. that afternoon to a late hour at night the enemy's sharpshooters, armed with Lee-Metford rifles and firing from very long ranges, sent bullet after bullet into the crowded camp.

The march was resumed the next day, the 13th. Brigadier-General Kempster's Brigade led the advance, the 4th Brigade bringing up the rear, and the transport moving between the brigades. To prevent the baggage of the 3rd and 4th Brigades getting mixed up, a whole regiment moved behind the 3rd Brigade baggage, and half a battalion at the head of the 4th Brigade. During this day there was heavier and more continuous fighting than at any previous time during the campaign, though the advanced guard of the 3rd Brigade was practically unmolested.

The enemy, emboldened by their successes of the day before, and their appetite whetted by the hope of still more plunder, showed a recklessness of danger which they had never hitherto displayed against absolutely unshaken and intact troops. The K.O.S.B.'s, the Royal Scots Fusiliers, the

Northamptonshire Regiment, the 1st Battalion 3rd Ghoorkhas, and the 36th Sikhs, all bore their share of the rearguard fighting, while the 1st Battalion 2nd Ghoorkhas and 2nd Punjaub Infantry guarded the flanks. The 36th Sikhs were commanded this day and the next by Major Des Vœux, Colonel Haughton being temporarily on the sick list.

Before the baggage had left camp, and while the K.O.S.B.'s and 1st Battalion 3rd Ghoorkhas were loading up, the enemy opened a heavy fire, killing ten of the animals. So accurate was their shooting that, as one man of the K.O.S.B.'s came in from picket and fell wounded, two more bullets struck him as he lay on the ground.

The valley for some little way just below the camp is wide; it then goes through a narrow gorge, and again broadens out till a place called Gali Khel is reached, some three miles from the camp, where the track to Swaikot, Brigadier-General Hammond's camp, leaves the river-bed. The banks of the stream-bed are quite half a mile apart in places; the river, swollen by the rain, had constantly to be crossed and re-crossed, and the morning was bitterly cold, though the sun shone out later in the day.

The transport drivers and followers, frightened by the noise of the constant firing behind them, and by the whizz of bullets passing above them, again lost their heads completely, and despite the fact that there were one and a half regiments between the 3rd and 4th Brigade baggage, the drivers pushed wildly forward. Up to the first gorge the baggage of the brigades could be kept apart; but once past it, the 4th Brigade baggage spread out in all directions, like a pent-up stream which has just burst its dam, and notwithstanding all the efforts made to keep it back, forced its way up into that of the 3rd Brigade, and the whole became inextricably mingled.

A temporary halt had to be made at Gali Khel to enable the road leading up from the stream to be improved, and the mass of transport had to halt while this was being done. Some 200 spare animals were loaded up with forage at a homestead halfway between the camp and Gali Khel; but no sooner had the laden animals joined the flood of transport which was sweeping along in the valley below, than load after load of forage was brushed off by the jostling crowd of animals as the valley began to narrow. What was not knocked off was pulled off and eaten by the other animals near, so that hardly a load reached the next camp intact. Meanwhile the troops on rear-guard, steady as if on parade, and personally directed and encouraged by Brigadier-General Westmacott, kept the swarming enemy at bay. As the head of the column, followed by the baggage, was seen to be leaving the river-bed and making for its new camp, which lay some five miles ahead at a place called Narkandai, the tribesmen, afraid that what they deemed their prey in the shape of the baggage would escape them, made a determined effort to cross the river and the valley and attack the transport on its left flank as it wound up from the river.

During the halt in the river-bed some of the transport drivers made desperate efforts to leave it at places where no laden animals could pass. Several men tried to drag their leading mules over a stone wall, and if they succeeded in doing so went on with the one mule, leaving two behind, and only too thankful to have a wall between them and the enemy's bullets. The tribesmen, however, did little or no damage to baggage animals or mule-drivers that day, for the troops on the rearguard and flanks fearlessly held them back.

A large number of the foe made a rush across the stream to try and effect their purpose of taking the baggage in flank, and came quite suddenly and unexpectedly under a cross fire, from the K.O.S.B.'s and a machine gun on the one bank and from the 3rd Ghoorkhas on the other. Many a tribesman threw up his arms in the water and floated down the stream a corpse, and the baggage, now that all was clear in front, wound up the road from the river.

From early morning till dusk it was one continual fight; regiments temporarily ran short of ammunition, and the killed and wounded were a great encumbrance, especially as the native dhooly-bearers had now ceased to even attempt to carry them.

There was no hurry, no hesitation, no mistake. The road, after leaving the river, ran through some undulating, and in places very broken ground, covered everywhere with low scrub jungle. The

3rd Brigade had halted some five miles from the river, and the 4th Brigade camp was formed a little behind it. As the rearguard, under Brigadier-General Westmacott, left the river, the towers and fortified houses far back along the valley, which had been fired as our troops passed them, sent clouds of smoke up into the air. The heavy losses which the enemy had suffered as they crossed the open valley under a deadly fire, and the destruction of every tower and loopholed house from Dwatoi to Gali Khel compensated in a large measure for our losses of the 11th.

Once the rearguard started to move through the scrub jungle, the enemy took advantage of every bush to creep up unseen. As dusk drew on Brigadier-General Westmacott's force had been so reduced by casualties, and still more so by the fighting men who had to carry their wounded comrades, that only two hundred of the Northampton Regiment, and about one hundred and fifty each of the K.O.S.B.'s, Royal Scots Fusiliers, 36th Sikhs, and 3rd Ghoorkhas, and a wing of the 1st Battalion 2nd Ghoorkhas were left on rearguard.

To have moved on in the fast-growing darkness to where the main column had encamped some two miles ahead would have involved still heavier losses, and the General decided to halt and spend the night on a ridge close by. The troops had occupied this position, and tired men were just beginning to sit down and rest after the heavy day, when the enemy made a most determined rush. The men were in their places in a moment; a withering fire was poured into the yelling tribesmen, and the troops had again shown that they were invincible. The foe seemed to melt away before this fire, but our troops suffered too; and when the smoke had cleared off it was seen that Lieutenant West, the gallant adjutant of the 1st Battalion 3rd Ghoorkhas, foremost in every fight, had fallen dead, with a bullet through his heart.

The troops who had thus held the enemy at bay, and had repulsed this last desperate rush with such stern determination, have good cause to be proud of their deeds; for never had the enemy fought more determinedly, and never were they more favoured by the ground. Not a mule or a follower was cut off; and though our losses were one officer killed and three wounded, and about twenty-four men killed and eighty wounded, the enemy had learnt a lesson. When he again followed up and harassed the retreat next day, it was in a very different manner from the day before, when caution had been thrown to the winds.

The wounded officers on the 13th were Captain Bateman Champain, 1st Battalion 3rd Ghoorkhas, slightly wounded, and Captain Short, Royal Scots Fusiliers, and Lieutenant Sellar, K.O.S.B.'s, severely wounded.

Although the head of the 3rd Brigade met with little or no resistance during the march from Sher Khel, the flanking parties thrown out by it, both on the 13th and 14th, materially assisted the march of the other brigade, and especially so that of the sorely pressed rearguard. On the evening of the 13th, the four or five companies of the 1st Battalion 2nd Ghoorkhas, who had been helping the 2nd Punjaub Infantry to hold the heights on the flanks, joined Brigadier-General Westmacott's rearguard as dusk came on, and remained with it during the night.

As the head of the 3rd Brigade reached camp

they were met by an advance guard from Brigadier-General Hammond's column, who had brought with them a large number of dhoolies and bearers to assist in carrying our wounded into Swaikot.

The camp at Narkandai was absolutely without water; men and followers had been cautioned to fill up their bottles before leaving the river. Most of them, it is true, had obeyed orders, but the contents of a single water bottle do not go far towards allaying the thirst of a man who has fought continuously all day, and who would have to fight for another five miles the next day before again obtaining a supply. The case of those who had neglected this advice was, of course, much worse.

The march was resumed early next morning, the 3rd Brigade leading the advance, and helping to protect the flanks, while the 4th Brigade again covered the movement. Nearly all the wounded had to be carried by their comrades; but the fresh dhooly-bearers from Swaikot were of some help.

The enemy, after their severe losses of the previous day, were far more cautious, and, though many men fell before their admirable long-range shooting, there was no more fighting at close quarters.

About four miles from Swaikot the troops of Brigadier-General Hammond's column were met with; their presence helped to take the pressure off the rearguard, and at 5 P.M. the troops of both brigades of the 2nd Division were safe in the new camp at Swaikot. The troops of this division sorely needed a rest, for on them had fallen, so far, the brunt of the losses during the campaign.

The troops of the 1st Division who marched down through the Orakzai country, and the troops of Brigadier-General Hammond's column, were in magnificent condition, and only too eager to try conclusions with the enemy; and while they afterwards moved up into the Khyber and Bazar valley, the 2nd Division troops enjoyed the rest they so greatly required.

It is not my purpose to pursue the narrative of the operations further than the arrival of the 1st and 2nd Divisions on the lower Bara river, the march through Tirah being the portion of the campaign with which I have attempted to deal.

This chapter, however, would not be complete without reference to the extremely successful march of the 1st Division, under Major-General Symons, down the Mastura Valley, and the sudden dash of the 1st Brigade into the Warān Valley.

The move of the 1st Division from Mastura began on the 8th December, in so far as the 1st Brigade and most of the Divisional troops were concerned. The force marched in two columns, Major-General Symons accompanying that which marched by the river, and Brigadier-General Hart commanding the one which moved north of the river. Snow and rain were falling as the troops moved off, and continued for seven hours, and it was bitterly cold work fording the Mastura stream.

Camp was formed at a spot about ten miles down the river, and reconnaissances were made of the valley ahead, and of the junction of the Warān and Mastura valleys, for the troops had now reached an unknown country

The next day some of the troops with the baggage moved on another six miles down the river, while a force under Brigadier-General Hart, consisting of the Derbyshire Regiment (95th), the Devonshire Regiment (11th), the 1st Ghoorkhas, the 30th Punjaub Infantry, the 21st Madras Pioneers, the Nabha Imperial Service Infantry, and No. 1 British and No. 1 Kohat Mountain Batteries, made a dash from the camp over a low pass into the Warān Valley.

It will be remembered that when Brigadier-General Kempster's column visited this valley on the 13th November, remaining till the 16th, that the Aka Khels' towers and houses had been spared, as this tribe up to the 15th, at all events, did not engage in hostilities against us: but the house of the pestilential Mullah, Sayad Akbar, and the towers of a section of the Zakka Khel tribe, who also inhabit the Warān Valley, were thoroughly destroyed. The Aka Khel tribe had, however, most undoubtedly joined the Zakka Khels in attacking the rearguard of Brigadier-General Kempster's column on the 16th, and it was desirable that they should be punished for this.

The surprise inflicted on the inhabitants of the valley was most complete. When the head of the column under Brigadier-General Hart appeared on the crest of the range of hills above the valley, the inhabitants in the case of the Zakka Khel section were busy repairing their dwellings, and Sayad Akbar's house had in a large measure been reconstructed.

Major-General Symons and his Staff watched the operations below from the top of the pass, and helped to expedite the movement of the force down into the valley below.

Every tower and loopholed house for a length of three miles was burnt or blown up, and the Mullah's house again completely demolished. The enemy fired from various points of vantage, but Brigadier-General Hart directed the operations with the greatest skill. The troops retired through each other alternately, so that no undue share of fighting or fatigue fell to any regiment: the batteries greatly assisted; and though Zakka Khels from other parts of Maidan came and joined in the fight, the troops repulsed every attack and got into their new camping ground near the junction of the Warān and Mastura valleys by 6.30 P.M.

Great loss had been inflicted on the enemy,

and immense damage done to their towers and houses; but so admirably had the troops been handled, that only one man was killed and four men and one follower wounded. The same day Brigadier-General Gaselee with his brigade (the 2nd) followed the 1st Brigade and encamped on the ground which the latter had vacated that morning.

The 1st Brigade moved next day (the 10th) further down the Mastura Valley to Barand Khel, the position of which is approximately shown on the map, and which is situated close to the foot of the then quite unknown and unexplored Sapri Pass. Brigadier-General Gaselee's brigade meanwhile closed up to within three miles. The 11th was spent in improving the road up to the pass, which was found to be very difficult. Constant snow and rain fell this day, and greatly added to the discomfort of the troops, while forage for the animals was almost unprocurable.

On the 12th December at 5 A.M. began the move of the 1st Brigade and of the Divisional troops over the Sapri Pass to Sapri village, ten miles distant. Rocks had constantly to be blasted, and the passage of the troops, and more especially of the baggage, was greatly delayed in consequence, and a large proportion of both had to spend the night on or just beyond the pass. Once over it the road was a little easier, and ran through a well-wooded ravine to Sapri village, a descent of 2,500 feet.

There was but little opposition, and on the 12th some of the 1st Brigade reached Swaikot. On the 13th Major-General Symons and the Divisional troops followed.

It was most important to get the whole of the transport of the 1st Brigade and Divisional troops over so as not to block the 2nd Brigade next day, for the latter was only rationed up to the 14th, while its transport animals had been on even shorter commons than those of the 1st Brigade. To expedite the movement of the baggage through the pass and the defile, Brigadier-General Hart, having first picketed all the surrounding heights, had large fires lit at intervals along the road. By the light of these, for wood was fortunately plentiful, the transport was able to move along the difficult road far on into the night. Although the Afridis offered no combined opposition, single sharpshooters considerably harassed the column at times, the 30th Punjaub Infantry of the 1st Brigade, who had been on duty continuously for thirty hours, keeping them at bay.

The General Officer commanding the 1st Brigade was indefatigable in his efforts to see that there was no unnecessary block on the pass, and remained on it until every man and animal of his brigade was safely across. Brigadier-General Gaselee followed close after, and by the 14th the whole of the 1st Division had reached Swaikot, and had begun to move off to their various camps.

Orakzai and Afridi Tirah had now been completely vacated by our troops; but though Sir William Lockhart, in the proclamation made to the Afridis before quitting Bagh, expressly averred that we were only leaving the country to avoid the snow, and that we should return, if necessary, in the spring, the mullahs and priests doubtless persuaded the tribesmen that our retirement was due to fear. This is probably the reason why the Kuki Khels, and more especially the Zakka Khels, so persistently impeded our march. Possibly the wiser men among them knew that we should harass their winter settlements and return to Tirah in the spring if our terms were not agreed to, but their advice would be outweighed by the mullahs, who pervert the Koran to suit their own views, and arouse the religious fanaticism of the people.

The total casualties in the march down the Bara Valley were one British officer killed and five wounded, and about 34 men killed and 140 wounded, without counting followers.

The total casualties from the commencement of the Tirah Expedition till the 14th December, when my narrative ends, were approximately as follows:—

	Killed.	Wounded.
British officers	17	41
Native officers	5	12
British rank and file	80	292
Native rank and file	137	345

It will doubtless be observed what a large proportion the number of officers killed and wounded bears to that of the men, showing not only how skilled was the enemy's marksmanship, but how gallantly at all times officers, both British and native, led their men on.

CHAPTER XIII.

RESULTS OF THE EXPEDITION AND FUTURE POLICY.

I PROPOSE in this last chapter to discuss with great briefness the military and political situation in regard to the Afridis, and to mention a few points where the Indian military organisation, excellent though it is as a whole, is still capable of some slight improvements.

After the close of the last Afghan War it was deemed of great importance that we should preserve for ourselves a right of way through the Khyber, the principal pass leading to Kabul, and through which an excellent military road had been made. In order to keep this pass open, an agreement was made in 1881 with the Afridis, through whose country for the most part it goes, by which we should pay them a yearly subsidy, and maintain a corps of Afridis, termed the Khyber Rifles. The latter force was to hold the pass, protect travellers and caravans, and help to guard our line of communications if at any time we wished to pass an army through the Khyber; and various posts along the pass were built at great expense by the Indian Government, and garrisoned by the Khyber Rifles.

So loyal was this corps deemed, that in 1888 we employed part of them in our expedition of that year against the Black Mountain tribes. They were at first commanded by Major Aslam Khan, an Afridi himself, while Colonel Warburton, who possesses an immense influence over the tribes, held the post of political officer in the Khyber. Everything appeared to work, and did no doubt work very smoothly, but the mechanism had not so far been very severely tested.

Some eighteen months ago Captain Barton, of ne Guides Cavalry, succeeded both Major Aslam Khan as Commandant, and Colonel Warburton (who had retired) as political officer, and continued to fulfil their joint duties with great success.

In August, 1897, a wave of fanaticism swept along the whole North-West Frontier of India, and rumours arose of intended attacks on the Khyber. Captain Barton therefore laid in supplies of food, water, and ammunition, increased the garrison of

Lundi Kotal, and decided to himself remain at the last-named fort. On the 17th August he heard on reliable authority that the Afridis had risen, and he sent to the Commissioner of Peshawur asking for a reinforcement of British troops. That official, however, did not deem it expedient to accede to the request, and ordered him on the 18th to come down to Jamrud, near the entrance to the pass on the British side. The Afridis attacked the forts on the 23rd August; and though the Khyber Rifles in some cases, and especially so at Lundi Kotal, fought bravely, without any British officer to direct them, fort after fort was taken or surrendered, and the whole pass fell into the hands of the Afridis, together with some rifles and fifty thousand rounds of ammunition.

There was, meanwhile, a column of our troops at Jamrud and another at Bara, but it was deemed advisable not to send them up the pass. The Commissioner of Peshawur had, doubtless, reasons of his own for not holding on to the Khyber, but the fact remains that our levies, armed, clothed, and paid by us, were left to their fate, and that, with the loss of the Khyber, a great blow had been dealt to our prestige. On the other hand, it has been argued that if detachments of our regular troops had been hastily sent up to the forts, these troops might have been blockaded and starved out, in which case the blow to our prestige would have been even greater. One thing is quite clear, and that is that the system attempted of trying to keep the pass open by means of a subsidy and paid levies broke down completely, and the question now presents itself as to how the Khyber Pass is to be held in the future.

The campaign against the Orakzais has been a complete success; it can hardly be said to have been so in the case of the Afridis. When the force started from Kohat there was a general expectation that the expedition would be over by about the 15th of December. It is now nearly the end of February, and still the majority of the tribes, and especially the Zakka Khels, remain recalcitrant, and a spring campaign appears far from improbable.

The Afridis have been told that they must hand in eight hundred breechloading rifles, in addition to a money fine. The question is, Will they do so even if we have a spring campaign? Let us consider for a moment what damage we have done them. We have eaten up a large quantity of their forage and grain, we have burnt their towers and fortified houses, we have used up a large amount of timber as firewood, and destroyed a great many trees. In very few cases have they attempted hand-to-hand fighting. When they have done so, they have lost heavily. They have, as a rule, fought, and fought to perfection, a guerilla warfare, in which we have lost heavily, and they have suffered, comparatively speaking, but little. Probably the total losses on their side do not amount to as many as on ours, more especially if we were to include our followers, who suffered so heavily in the march down the Bara Valley.

If we return to Tirah in the spring we shall feed our animals on the spring crops, and again destroy any towers which have been rebuilt, and probably prevent the sowing of the autumn crops. The old men, the women, and the children among the tribes will feel the want of food severely; but the young men, the fighting men, in whom the lust for murder, plunder, and revenge is the strongest, will probably be only too glad to continue a guerilla warfare from which our troops, no matter how brave and skilful and how well led, must suffer considerably.

It is these young men in reality whom we are asking to hand up their rifles, which are worth, to them, almost their actual weight in silver, and which they have in most instances risked their lives to obtain. Many men who have captured rifles in addition to those they owned before, will have sold them to neighbouring tribesmen, and their recovery is impossible. It must be remembered, too, that once a man has handed up his rifle he is no longer able to defend himself or to prosecute the numerous blood feuds for which the Afridis are so famous.

Let us suppose for a moment, however, that we do bring sufficient pressure to bear on the tribesmen to induce them to part with their rifles. A tremendous amount of life and money will have been spent, and what guarantee have we but that in a few years the expedition will have to be repeated with just as much loss and expense as before? In any case, whenever we want to use the Khyber Pass, we shall have an implacable foe on our flanks, burning to avenge the loss and damage we have done them, ready to turn on us the moment they deem the favourable opportunity has arisen, and rendering the protection of our line of communications most difficult and dangerous.

Even in times of peace, the Khyber Pass, if we garrison it ourselves, will be liable to attack, and it is not improbable but that a flying column will have to be maintained on a war footing at Peshawur, prepared at any moment to reinforce the garrisons in the pass.

To many people who are intimately acquainted with the frontier tribes there seems to be but one permanent remedy, and that is annexation. The Government of India have already decided against this on the score of expense, and even if they had been in favour of it, it is extremely doubtful if the English Government would have given its consent.

The idea has largely gained ground that our so-called forward policy has been the cause of many of our small wars, and there seems a large amount of truth in the suggestion.

Had the line of the Indus been finally adopted as the North-West Frontier of India we might possibly have left all the tribes beyond the Indus, including the Afghans, to their own devices. This policy would doubtless have succeeded admirably if only Afghanistan and the frontier tribes had to be reckoned with; but when a great European Power, whose territory is always expanding, and who possesses most successful methods of subjugating savage or semi-barbarous nations, drew nearer and nearer to the north of Afghanistan, quite a different policy was rendered necessary. Passive defence behind a river line, especially with a country in rear which might welcome an invader, is well known to be one of the greatest military errors which can be perpetrated, and history, as far as I know, records no instance of the successful defence of a river line, or of a campaign being won by purely passive defence.

For this and other reasons our frontier line was pushed beyond the Indus, and from time to time, of late years, fortified posts have been established beyond our frontier line to enable us to use various routes on which they are situated, should we wish to do so. The establishment of these posts has been a somewhat doubtful policy, and those in the Malakand and on the Samana range were very severely attacked in the summer of '97. Some people have attributed all our troubles solely to this forward policy, and to the establishment and retention of these advanced posts; but they forget the wave of Mahommedan fanaticism caused by the Turkish successes over the Greeks.

To all intents and purposes, our endeavour to hold the Khyber Pass by advanced posts has signally failed. How are we going to hold it now? If we post our own troops up there we shall, in all probability, have the same experiences as we had at the Malakand and on the Samana. The establishment of these posts appears, and very naturally so, to the surrounding tribes as a standing menace and insult, and sooner or later fresh troubles will arise and more expensive expeditions will ensue.

It seems, therefore, worth considering if the annexation of Afridi Tirah, together with the Khyber Pass, would not in the end be cheaper than constant expeditions, and I propose to mention some of the moral and strategical advantages which would result from such a step.

Sir William Lockhart's proclamation to the Afridis said that *if* we were not opposed, the country would not be annexed. We *have* been opposed at every turn, so the promise is no longer binding. The moral effect on all the tribes of the North-West Frontier if we annexed the country of the Afridis because they had committed themselves would be enormous; for if we showed our ability to take and hold the country of the most powerful, most numerous, and most wealthy tribe on the border, other tribes, inhabiting a country much more accessible than Tirah, and able to offer far less resistance than the Afridis, would probably hesitate and finally decline to listen to any priest or agitator who urged them to rise against us. To annex the Afridi country would, it is true, involve a very large initial expenditure. Forts would have to be built, a light railway made, and large supplies kept in store in case the line of communications was interfered with.

If the Afridis declined to return and cultivate the soil, for the produce of which we should of course pay them, Sikh or other cultivators could be called in, and would have the protection of the forts to retire to at night. The Afridis are not a more warlike race than were the Sikhs, whose country we successfully annexed, and who have ever since been our staunchest allies. Before long, in all probability (and I am now quoting not my own opinion, but that of one of the most experienced and successful political officers on the frontier), the Afridis, provided only they were not interfered with in domestic matters nor subjected to all the sections of the Indian penal code, would settle down and contentedly reap the great pecuniary advantages to be derived from trading with us.

In dealing with them, political officers of very great tact would be required, for there have been cases in which the tribesmen's customs in regard to domestic habits have been meddled with, and this is a sure cause of trouble. Local corps, like the Khyber Rifles, could be formed, enlistment into which would be most popular, for no Afridi likes serving very far from his home. Living, as the men of these local, or partly local, corps would do, with their wives and families round them, they would gradually bring influence to bear on other members of their families or of their tribe.

The Afridi is almost as fond of money as of fighting, and once he began to acquire money and possessions he would gradually come to see that the preservation of order would be for the common good. In this manner they would gradually be disarmed, for those who would not settle down and hand in or dispose of their rifles, would not easily find a home elsewhere; our troops, in strong forts, would be safe against any attack if a good water supply was always laid in, and it would be to the interest of all those who had land in the near neighbourhood of the forts to give us timely notice of any rising or threatened disturbances.

The strategical advantages of annexing Tirah are enormous. Just as Metz, with its immensely strong fortifications forming an entrenched camp, has been compared to a dagger held at the heart of France, so would our position be in Tirah towards any force seeking to invade India. It is nowadays generally admitted that, in the event of complications with Russia, and an attempt by her to invade India, our policy must be to fight her beyond the North-West Frontier, and to do so we ought to be in a position to seize Kandahar and Kabul. Kandahar we can very quickly reach from Quetta; Kabul can be easily arrived at either by the Kurram Valley or by the Khyber route, but in either case the line of communications is a long one, and if the Afridis were hostile it would be far from secure, for their country lies between the two routes. If Tirah were held, however, it would serve as an advanced depôt, or even as a base, and far in advance of either Peshawur or Kohat, with both of which it could be connected by a light railway.

The country is very rich and would help to supply the needs of an army. There is no direct route from Afghanistan into Tirah from the westward and north-westward, and the country is therefore not open to invasion on that side. If, however, a British force was operating from Tirah, it could, securely based itself, act against the flank or lines of communication of a force invading India by either the Kurram or the Khyber, and that without the least fear of being cut off, as it would have a secure line of retreat between the two other routes; it would in fact be working on "interior lines."

No army trying to invade India either by the Kurram or the Khyber, or by both, could afford to neglect a force in Tirah; if it did, its line of communications would be cut. The Tirah force would have to be "masked," or held back, or operated against and defeated, before the main advance could be resumed. Such are some of the moral and strategical advantages which the occupation of Tirah would secure us. The objection is that the cost would be enormous. This is quite true, but would it be as enormous as the cost of constant frontier expeditions, and is our prestige not worth the expense?

Another objection urged against it is that the Indian Army is already as large as the country can possibly afford, and that if we occupied Tirah, a permanent addition would be necessary. The number of troops required, however, might be supplied by reductions elsewhere; that is to say, certain regiments which are not composed of good fighting material, and which are only useful for police purposes, might be disbanded, and others of better material might be quartered on the frontier, while certain stations in India which have no turbulent population might be left ungarrisoned.

Nearly all officers who have had much dealing with the Afridis are convinced that even if they do eventually submit and make terms the snake will have been scotched and not killed, and that they will always remain our implacable foes. In regard to this it may be urged that if we occupy Tirah, and the Afridis gradually settle down, there will still be no finality, as we shall then have complications with the Afghan tribes beyond.

It is possible of course that this might happen, but we should then be dealing with a race of people who do recognise a ruler. The Afridis recognise none; and it would be to the interests of the Amir of Afghanistan, to whom we pay a large yearly subsidy, that his subjects should not cross our border. The Amir, moreover, has methods of dealing with refractory tribesmen, which, though opposed to Western ideas, are most efficacious; and his power is much respected in consequence.

Annexation is, however, out of favour at this moment; forward policy and any increase of responsibility have been held up to public obloquy, and the question of annexation will not perhaps at the present time be considered on its merits, much as there may be to recommend it. Time only will show.

If any other means can be taken to permanently pacify the Afridis, to make the Khyber and the

Kurram secure routes, and to avoid frontier expeditions, then annexation is by all means to be deprecated, even with its strategical advantages.

If, however, in future years, there are constant disturbances, it will probably appear that the cost of the expeditions to punish them would have been sufficient for the annexation and holding of Tirah.

I will now, in conclusion, mention a few points in which, excellent though the organisation and equipment of the Indian Army is on the whole, as the campaign in Tirah has shown, there is still room for improvement. Dealing first with the transport, it seemed to be the opinion of all the Commissariat and Transport officers that the provision of a light railway along the line of communication, when the latter is on fairly level ground, would be an immense boon and ultimately save expense. The enormous mortality, too, among ponies and donkeys, and the manner in which their unsuitability for pack transport affected the mobility of the force, seems to show the great desirability for the provision of a much larger mule transport.

Closely connected with the transport question

comes that of the hospital equipment. Medical officers, speaking with experience of the field hospitals in England or on the Continent, declared our Indian hospital equipment to be very heavy and cumbrous, and that it required much more transport than would otherwise be necessary. Nearly all the drugs used are in liquid form, whereas compressed drugs in tabloids would be infinitely better suited to field service, saving much time and trouble in compounding and enormously decreasing the weight. The use of aluminium, too, instead of heavier metal, would be a great saving.

Fortunately for all wounded men who had been hit by bullets which could not easily be extracted, Surgeon-Major Beevor, Army Medical Staff, who has been attached for some years to the Brigade of Guards, obtained permission to come out to India for a year, and bring with him his Röntgen Ray apparatus. With this, which he had purchased at his own expense, he joined one of the field hospitals, and was enabled in many cases to show the exact position of a bullet whose course could not be followed. In one instance, a soldier, wearing a sheepskin coat, was hit by a bullet, which, as it entered the man's body, took with it a complete envelope of sheepskin. The medical officer, probing for the bullet, consequently felt a soft object which he did not think was the bullet; the Röntgen Rays at once showed that this soft object was really the covering of the bullet, and enabled it to be easily extracted. The negative results, too, were excellent, inasmuch as it showed at once if there was any foreign substance in a wound.

As it was purely due to private enterprise that so many wounded men's sufferings were alleviated, and that limbs which would otherwise have been amputated were in many cases spared, a Röntgen Ray apparatus would seem to be a very great addition to the medical equipment of a force.

So far, possibly because a deterioration takes place in the Indian climate, compressed rations or soup have not yet been supplied to soldiers on service in India. There were many occasions in Tirah when the men spent bitterly cold nights with little or nothing to eat because the baggage had not come up. Every German soldier carries his "iron ration," containing in a compressed form enough food for a day, and if soup tabloids are carried, a bowl of hot soup, to a man cold and tired, is an immense boon. It is therefore to be hoped that a compressed ration of food or soup, which will stand the Indian climate, will soon be introduced.

Lastly, it is much to be hoped that the Indian military authorities may see their way to increase the number of Ghoorkha scouts in future campaigns, for the service rendered to the whole force by the scouts of the 3rd and 5th Ghoorkhas can hardly be over-estimated. Their total number was under one hundred, and, though they were constantly engaged, and killed large numbers of the enemy, their own casualties were very small. Led by Captain Lucas and Lieutenants Bruce and Tillard these scouts would climb a mountain side with the most astonishing rapidity, and, either in action by day, or when intercepting and capturing tribesmen who were shooting into our camp at night, they were more than equal to the Pathans in mobility, cunning and bravery.

I have mentioned a few points in which, in the

opinion of most officers with the Tirah force, the Indian army organisation might still further be improved; but when one takes into consideration the large force engaged, it is wonderful how well everything worked. The concentration of the troops at Kohat both by rail and road was effected smoothly and quickly; there was no lack of supplies, the quality of the food was good, the troops were well and warmly clothed, and the medical arrangements for treating the wounded and sending back sick men to the base worked admirably. Some of the transport was at first very inefficient, but as time went on the weakly animals were replaced by stronger ones, and much was due to the unremitting efforts of the Commissariat and Transport Department.

Although the Afridis have not yet all submitted to the terms we wished to impose (the conditions of which are more severe than any hitherto demanded from a frontier tribe) we have nevertheless shown both Afridis and Orakzais that we are able to penetrate into the recesses of Tirah, which, it was their boast, had never before been invaded.

Our losses, it is true, have been heavy, but this was inevitable with an enemy who would not risk a stand-up fight, and who inhabit a most difficult country, who are certainly the finest skirmishers in the world, and who fight a guerilla warfare to perfection.

Of one thing we may rest quite certain—namely, that no other troops in the world could have fought a better campaign. The conditions of the country, of the weather, and of the nature of the fighting rendered it one of the most severe and demoralising that our armies have ever been engaged in; yet the troops of the Tirah Field Force, both British and native, were always cheerful and uncomplaining, and exhibited a dogged courage that not only deserved, but commanded, the success they ultimately attained.

APPENDIX.

Composition of the Tirah Field Force.

THE MAIN COLUMN.

First Division.

First Brigade.

2nd Battalion, The Derbyshire Regiment.
1st Battalion, The Devonshire Regiment.
2nd Battalion, 1st Ghoorkhas.
30th Punjaub Infantry.
No. 6 British Field Hospital.
No. 34 Native Field Hospital.

Second Brigade.

2nd Battalion, The Yorkshire Regiment.
1st Battalion, Royal West Surrey Regiment.
2nd Battalion, 4th Ghoorkhas.
3rd Sikhs.
Sections A and B of No. 8 British Field Hospital.
Sections A and C of No. 14 British Field Hospital.
No. 31 Native Field Hospital.

Divisional Troops.

No. 1 Mountain Battery, Royal Artillery.
No. 2 (Derajat) Mountain Battery.
No. 1 (Kohat) Mountain Battery.
Two Squadrons, 18th Bengal Lancers.

Appendix. 317

28th Bombay Infantry (Pioneers).
No. 3 Company, Bombay Sappers and Miners.
No. 4 Company, Bombay Sappers and Miners.
One Printing Section from the Bombay Sappers and Miners.
The Kapurthala Regiment of Imperial Service Infantry.
The Maler Kotla Imperial Service Sappers.
Section A of No. 13 British Field Hospital.
No. 63 Native Field Hospital.

SECOND DIVISION.

Third Brigade.

1st Battalion, The Gordon Highlanders.
1st Battalion, The Dorsetshire Regiment.
1st Battalion, 2nd Ghoorkhas.
15th Sikhs.
No. 24 British Field Hospital.
No. 44 Native Field Hospital.

Fourth Brigade.

2nd Battalion, The King's Own Scottish Borderers.
1st Battalion, The Northamptonshire Regiment.
1st Battalion, 3rd Ghoorkhas.
36th Sikhs.
Sections C and D of No. 9 British Field Hospital.
Sections A and B of No. 23 British Field Hospital.
No. 48 Native Field Hospital.

Divisional Troops.

No. 8 Mountain Battery, Royal Artillery.
No. 9 Mountain Battery, Royal Artillery.
No. 5 (Bombay) Mountain Battery.
Machine Gun Detachment, 16th Lancers.
Two Squadrons, 18th Bengal Lancers.
21st Madras Infantry (Pioneers).
No. 4 Company, Madras Sappers and Miners.
One Printing Section from the Madras Sappers and Miners.

The Jhind Regiment of Imperial Service Infantry.
The Sirmur Imperial Service Sappers.
Section B of No. 13 British Field Hospital.
No. 43 Native Field Hospital.

LINE OF COMMUNICATION TROOPS.

22nd Punjaub Infantry.
2nd Battalion, 2nd Ghoorkhas.
39th Garhwal Rifles.
2nd Punjaub Infantry.
3rd Bengal Cavalry.
No. 42 Native Field Hospital.
No. 52 Native Field Hospital.
The Jeypore Imperial Service Transport Corps.
The Gwalior Imperial Service Transport Corps.
Ordnance Field Park.
Engineer Field Park.
British General Hospital, of 500 Beds, at Rawalpindi
Native General Hospital, of 500 Beds, at Rawalpindi
No. 1 Field Medical Store Depôt.
No. 2 Field Medical Store Depôt.
No. 5 Veterinary Field Hospital.
No. 11 British Field Hospital.
No. 25 British Field Hospital.
No. 47 Native Field Hospital.
No. 64 Native Field Hospital.

THE PESHAWAR COLUMN.

2nd Battalion, The Royal Inniskilling Fusiliers.
2nd Battalion, The Oxfordshire Light Infantry.
9th Ghoorkhas.
45th Sikhs.
57th Field Battery, Royal Artillery.
No. 3 Mountain Battery, Royal Artillery.
9th Bengal Lancers.
No. 5 Company, Bengal Sappers and Miners.

Appendix.

No. 5 British Field Hospital.
No. 45 Native Field Hospital.
British General Hospital, of 250 Beds.
Native General Hospital, of 500 Beds.

THE KURRAM MOVEABLE COLUMN.

12th Bengal Infantry.
The Nabha Regiment of Imperial Service Infantry.
4 Guns, 3rd Field Battery, Royal Artillery.
6th Bengal Cavalry.
One Regiment Central India Horse.
Section D of No. 3 British Field Hospital.
No. 62 Native Field Hospital.
Section B of No. 46 Native Field Hospital.
Native General Hospital, of 200 Beds.

THE RAWALPINDI RESERVE BRIGADE.

2nd Battalion, The King's Own Yorkshire Light Infantry.
1st Battalion, The Duke of Cornwall's Light Infantry.
27th Regiment Bombay Infantry.
2nd Regiment of Infantry, Hyderabad Contingent.
Jodhpur Imperial Service Lancers.
No. 12 British Field Hospital.
No. 53 Native Field Hospital.

LIST OF AUTHORS.

	PAGE
Rudyard Kipling	17
Capt. M. H. Hayes, F.R.C.V.S.	6
L. G. Carr Laughton	10
Capt. L. J. Shadwell, P.S.C.	11
Henry O'Brien	13
M. Mookerjee	19
Vero Shaw	5
John Watson	4
E. Markwick	15
Fred T. Jane	10
Vety.-Major J. A. Nunn	5
E. H. Aitken	16
Lincoln Springfield	14
Hamlin Garland	15
D. C. Boulger	13
W. Laird Clowes	9
H. G. Keene, C.I.E.	19
J. G. Whyte Melville	3
Paul Cushing	15
General Kinloch	5
Major W. Yeldham	11
H. E. Busteed, C.I.E.	18
Alfred E. Pease, M.P.	3
H. S. Thomas, F.L.S.	22
E. D. Miller	7
Lady Violet Greville	4
Mrs. O'Donoghue	4
Col. H. M. S. Brunker	11
Daniel Brunn	12
Major Hamylton Fairleigh	15
Thacker's Industries of India	22
,, Indian Directory	21
,, Map of India	23

www.ingramcontent.com/pod-product-compliance
Lightning Source LLC
Chambersburg PA
CBHW032356230426
43672CB00007B/722